Lifelong
Love

ID0950569

Lifelong Love

4 Steps to Creating and Maintaining an Extraordinary Relationship

PHYLLIS KOCH-SHERAS, Ph.D.
& PETER SHERAS, Ph.D.

Lifelong Love

ISBN-13: 978-0-373-89238-9

Koch-Sheras, Phyllis R.
Lifelong Love: 4 steps to creating and maintaining an extraordinary relationship/Phyllis Koch-Sheras and Peter Sheras.
        p. cm.
ISBN 978-0-373-89238-9
1. Love. 2. Marriage. 3. Interpersonal relations. 4. Commitment (Psychology). 5. Intimacy (Psychology). I. Sheras, Peter L. II. Title.
HQ734.K6717 2012
302—dc23
        2012005895

4967 6660 9/12

www.Harlequin.com

Printed in U.S.A.

Contents

Contents

Part II: Creating Lifelong Love:
Building Couple Power with the Four C's

Part III: Challenges and Possibilities in Daily Life

Preface

It's pretty easy to fall in love. What seems harder and harder these days, however, is to stay there—to have lifelong love that is as fulfilling and exciting as those initial experiences were. As psychologists and as a married couple ourselves, we have been looking for the factors that explain this phenomenon. We have examined our own relationship, talked to others about it, done extensive research and worked with hundreds of couples. After more than thirty years, we have concluded that there are four simple, though not necessarily easy, steps to achieving lifelong love: commitment, cooperation, communication and community. The path to fulfilling these steps is described in the model we call "Couple Power."

Our personal and professional experiences, along with the observations and reports of our clients, friends and colleagues, have convinced us that this is an approach that really works and makes a huge difference for couples. Having already written a book for couples therapists and having taught the Couple Power Therapy

(CPT) model to many of them, we were encouraged to bring Couple Power to the world. So here it is. Power to the couple!

We are aware that there are already many self-help books and articles about relationships out there. However, even the best ones haven't seemed to help very much. When we looked at them, we saw that most of these publications offer simplistic solutions that don't address the uniqueness of each couple. Generally, what you get is advice on how to figure out what's wrong with your relationship and how to fix it, rather than ways to create together positive visions and solutions for your relationship. Communication skills, while important, are usually taught before you are ready to make effective use of them. This can be dangerous, as this knowledge often makes things worse rather than better. Communication is a powerful tool, but only when individuals are equipped with proper directions on how and when to use it.

The Couple Power approach to creating lifelong love is different than conventional approaches, in that it helps couples build a relationship in which they work together as a unique entity, as a committed team, one that addresses problems together, while supporting and receiving help from other couples in the process. If all couples utilized the Couple Power approach, it wouldn't be long before there was a paradigm shift in how the world views the possibility of lifelong love for couples: the *norm* would be for couples to stay together in fulfilling and lasting relationships. Couples wouldn't tolerate each other or compromise just to survive; they would naturally support each other in maintaining and enhancing their relationships over time, and consequently, children of divorce would be the exception rather than the rule.

This vision for couples may sound unrealistic and even radical to you at this point in our history. We are a nation built on individualism, not "couplism." There is a natural tension between individualism and the kind of "collectivism" that a couple represents. What we show you in this book is how to bridge the gap between the two while embracing—and even enhancing—your individual goals in the context of "Couple," creating and maintaining lifelong love for yourself and others along the way. We are excited to begin the journey with you now.

There are several people who have helped us along the way, on our own journey to lifelong love. We would especially like to acknowledge our mentors at the Veterans Administration Hospital in Palo Alto, California, who gave us such rich and rigorous training on the Family Study Unit. Little did we know then that we would be applying that training to create lifelong love for our own relationship as well as for others. (We will discuss this in greater detail later in the book.) The organization Couples Coaching Couples, Inc., has also been instrumental in the development of our relationship and the ideas that led to the creation of the Couple Power model. We will always be active members of this organization. Many insightful people helped edit and refine this book, including Phyllis's faithful critique group from the Blue Ridge chapter of the Virginia Writers Club, our supportive agent, Mary Beth Chappell, our extraordinary editor, Deborah Brody and our very special assistant and friend, Linda Childs.

Special gratitude is due to all the clients we have seen over the decades. They are our most masterful teachers. In these chapters we have included numerous stories of their lives, disguising their identities for privacy's sake. We owe each of them great appreciation for making this book readable, accessible and, hopefully, enjoyable for you, the general reader. There is treasure in these pages. Read them as though you are looking for gold. We hope you enjoy the many riches available to you and your couple in all the years to come—all your life long.

Redefining What It Means to Be a Couple

CHAPTER ONE

Lifelong Love:

A Couple Is Greater Than the Sum of Its Parts

"Dance me to the end of love...."
—Leonard Cohen

As couples therapists who also happen to be married to each other, we are often asked how it is that our relationship has not only lasted for nearly forty years but has also thrived. Part of the answer may lie in the history of our relationship. We met after graduate school, when Phyllis was thirty and Peter was twenty-six. Phyllis had been married before and had been divorced for nearly a year when she met Peter, who, though he'd had some significant relationships since college, had not been in any that were very serious or long lasting. Despite some differences in our ages, circumstances and relationship histories, we fell deeply in love. At the time we were training to be family therapists, and both of us were totally immersed in learning about relationships. Together and separately, we'd spent innumerable hours studying and working with couples, helping them understand the dynamic between them and what was missing in the relationship they'd begun with such high hopes. But there was even more to it than that.

In a discussion of how our relationship blossomed, Peter noted, "About two months after we began dating, I noticed that my feelings for Phyllis had become quite strong. When I passed her in the hall at work, I would feel flushed." Phyllis reported sitting in a colleague's office one day when Peter walked past the open door. She had an intense reaction, which was obvious to her coworker, who asked, "What just happened? Who was that that just walked by?" The attraction between us was palpable, even to others. One day Peter was sitting in the cafeteria in the hospital where we worked when he saw Phyllis walk in. He imagined what it would be like to say to someone, "That's my wife!" In that instant, he saw the possibility of committing to a relationship and the couple known as "Phyllis and Peter" was born for him. For the first time, Peter could imagine a future lived as a couple.

Phyllis explained, "I saw Peter at the orientation meeting for my new job. I was actually not sure then if I was going to stay in the position, as I had another offer that I was thinking of taking instead. But after I saw Peter, there was no question that I'd remain. It was love at first sight for me, and the attraction I felt was undeniable. Although we didn't begin dating until a few months later, I had already started imagining a future with him. Newly divorced, I was thoroughly enjoying dating again. But as time went on, my newfound freedom began to pale in comparison to what I was feeling for Peter. This became especially clear after he had me over for dinner one night. He 'had me' at the clam sauce, but he really sealed the deal when he serenaded me on his guitar after dinner. That was it for those other guys I was dating."

Falling in love is the easy part, however. The challenge is how to keep that spark alive over time and achieve what we call lifelong love. We have been working on this professionally and personally for close to forty years now, and we have met and worked with other couples facing that same challenge. We have learned from them, from our mentors and from our own experience what it takes to make a relationship work and last.

Here we will share with you how we have sustained our lifelong love and enabled hundreds of other couples to do the same.

What Is Lifelong Love?

From the time we are teenagers, and maybe even before, we day-dream about love and relationships. We see love modeled by our parents or other adults when we are young. As we mature, we discover that we are surrounded by cultural images of love: they abound in the media, in romance novels and in music, in movies and on the internet. It is impossible to imagine growing up without entertaining notions of love and romance.

But what is love? What makes a relationship great or a marriage fulfilling? Is love a fantasy, an expectation, a moment, a sense of completion or one's destiny? Is love a pure feeling that is unexplainable, unpredictable, indescribable or miraculous? Do we find it or do we create it? Is it by chance or by our own force of will that we find our beloved? Once we find love, can we keep it? When we fall in love, how long do we expect it to last? Is our love meant to be forever or just until "the thrill is gone"? Is love constant or does it evolve over time? It seems that there are more questions about love than answers. This book helps answer these questions and describes the kind of love that creates profoundly fulfilling, lasting relationships.

Love sometimes seems like a moving target: we think we can recognize it, but we are never sure when or where it will appear or how to hold on to it. It is probably fair to say that our perception of love changes over time. While the subject of love is complex and confusing, we persist in clinging to the desire to be swept into the arms of our beloved, where we will live happily ever after. When love is new, we get caught up in the excitement of it and rarely bother to ask questions. At some point, however, we come back down to earth and ask ourselves what it will take to sustain this feeling. In answering this particular question, we will demonstrate how some people have accomplished lifelong love, and how others may have missed opportunities to do so along the way. One of the things we have discovered over the years is that lifelong love is less about having the right partner and more about creating the right relationship. Lifelong love is committing to a partnership that is made to last and to be enjoyed forever, even as the individuals change. It is not about constant compromise or "toughing it out." It is not just staying together for the sake of the children or for financial security or for other reasons. It is truly about being in a relationship that is fun and profoundly fulfilling.

Why Choose Lifelong Love?

Some may entertain the notion that finding one particular person to love forever has become obsolete. When contemplating an existing relationship, they may ask, "What if s/he is really not my 'soul's' true mate? What if another, better option shows up in my future?" The fact is that whenever a relationship breaks up, in addition to the emotional turmoil, there is the challenge of having to reconstruct one's life, often with the added heartache of a child-custody conflict.

There would appear to be many advantages to sticking with a long-term relationship with the same person, including a sense of security, predictability, intimacy, ease and just plain convenience. Lasting relationships provide emotional stability and comfort through a history of shared experiences. The sweep of our history together allows us to see the power of perseverance in overcoming obstacles and weathering crises side by side. A shared history, the same points of reference, anchors the story of our lives and fosters a strong bond between us.

In a long-term relationship, there develops familiarity, a deeper connection, a mirror in which to see yourself reflected, all of which have stood the test of time and events. Enduring relationships demonstrate the abiding nature of love in their hardiness and timeworn, unspoken acceptance. Such relationships also develop a resiliency, which increases the likelihood of longevity. They encompass and surpass both friendship and love: they are unique entities unto themselves. Finally, lifelong relationships nurture strong extended families that support parents as well as children.

Why Not Lifelong Love?

Given all the blessings that enduring relationships bestow, why would you choose anything other than lifelong love? Perhaps it's because you really don't want to be with the same person the rest of your life. Maybe you want more variety. Or you might be afraid that your partner will change in a way you don't like. Your concerns may be driven by a fear of the future; you may have misgivings about making such a long-term emotional investment in just one person. Can love really conquer all?

There are many fears that go hand in hand with the potential for joy in a lifelong relationship. Rarely do we dwell on these fears in the first heady days of infatuation; if unexamined, however, these fears have the capacity to sabotage us as we move through the later stages of a developing relationship. For instance, our concerns may influence our decision to commit to dating exclusively, to be physically intimate, to move in together, to invest or purchase things together, to share a pet, to get engaged and get married or to have children. In times of adversity, these fears drive us away from one another.

In our work with couples over the decades, we have seen many instances of this. Initially, there may be fears about getting into a relationship. The anticipation that something might go wrong can be a source of anxiety and hypervigilance. These fears are in large part overblown. For example, people's fear of abandonment vastly outweighs the likelihood of them actually being left. Sometimes the very fear itself gives rise to behavior that may lead to the feared thing coming to pass, resulting in a self-fulfilling prophecy. For example, "If I am afraid that you will push me away, I might not risk getting close to you, and the effect is that I am pushed away because I do not appear interested in being close."

Questions and myths about lifelong love

The following are some common questions and myths that cause many people to avoid committing to a relationship:

- **I am afraid I might have chosen the wrong person.** What if I find out later that s/he has a secret life or has been manipulating me to get something (sex, money, citizenship, protection)? Am I just being used? Could I be missing something crucial?
- **I am going to have to compromise.** Most everybody thinks that if you want to be in a relationship, you have to give

something up. What will I have to give up? What if it's something really important to me, like nights out with my girlfriends or afternoons on the golf course with my buddies?

- **What if the relationship becomes abusive?** Could I have missed some warning sign that this person could be verbally, physically or emotionally abusive down the road? Is there a problem with alcohol or drugs that I have ignored? How will I cope with the consequences of these unknowns?

- **I am not sure I am really in love with this person.** I might have been confusing infatuation with love when we first met. If this isn't really love, what am I going to do now? Can I stay in a relationship with someone I have never really loved? What if I find a better person later?

- **I can get hurt if I love too much.** What if I really give myself to the person I love and then s/he abandons me? If that happens, I will be devastated! I'd better always have an exit plan, a back door out of the relationship, just in case. . . .

- **This relationship might turn out to be really boring.** What if, years from now, we are just going through the motions of the same old routine, with nothing new or exciting happening? I am not sure I want to risk boredom for the rest of my life. I need challenge and variety, and if I can't find them inside my relationship, I may have to look outside. Work may be more satisfying, fulfilling and interesting than being stuck at home with my family.

- **This relationship is stifling.** This relationship takes too much time and work. I would rather be doing something more creative, something that is more a manifestation of my self-expression, of who I really am. If I stay in this relationship, I will never achieve my full potential and live my dreams.

- **If I am completely involved in a relationship with my partner, what happens to my sense of self?** We are supposed to be equal partners in this relationship. I am concerned that I am always trying to be the person my partner wants me to be, with no space to be my real self. If I am not being completely honest but I am always trying to please my partner, I will lose myself and will never be happy.
- **What if sometimes we are just too busy to work on our relationship?** Life can be a struggle, and we must both work long hours just to make ends meet. I hope our relationship is able to take care of itself out of our love for each other, because we are both too busy and exhausted to deal with it. Maybe I was better off when I was alone and was not responsible for so much.
- **I am stuck. What if I want to leave but can't because of finances or children or guilt?** Maybe painting myself into a corner by being in a relationship is not such a good idea. I may be in love now, but what if that fades, and I am stuck living in a place where I don't want to live?

Fears that drive us into a relationship

There are also fears that can drive us *into* a relationship and keep us there. These fears may make a commitment to lifelong love feel like a trap you cannot escape.

- **I am afraid of being alone.** I have never liked being alone, and I don't do well by myself. The reason I got into a relationship was not just love but also companionship. I need someone to provide for me, protect me and take care of me emotionally. I am not sure that I can manage on my own; sometimes I really need help navigating all the demands of my life.

- **I am lonely.** Sometimes I am so blue and lonesome. I really need someone to talk to; this may not be love, but at least it fills the awful emptiness of being alone, with no one with whom to share my life.
- **I need security.** I worry about money, resources and having a home for my family. A relationship can provide that for me, and maybe that is more important than being in love right now.
- **I really need protection.** I have had a tough life so far, and I am concerned that I am still not safe. I need someone who will look out for me, stand up for me and protect me. I have already been threatened, so this relationship could be a safe fortress against outside danger. I have escaped from abuse before, and I am afraid of being abused again. This relationship is my protection.
- **This is the best I can do.** It has been a long time since anyone has shown any interest in me, and I don't know if I will find the love of my life. Even though this relationship may not be the best, maybe this is as good as it gets, and I should lower my expectations. If I don't seize this opportunity, I may not have another one. Perhaps "a bird in the hand is worth two in the bush."

Is Lifelong Love Really Possible?

Given all our fears and our fantasies, is truly enjoyable lifelong love really possible, or does it exist only in fairy tales and romance novels? Fairy tales end happily ever after, but the divorce rate in most Western societies indicates that the reality is otherwise. More than half of all marriages fail, and many people in the other half stay in the relationship even though their marriage does not make them happy. The real question is, "If we want lifelong, fulfilling love, how do we achieve it?" We are going to show you how. After reading this book and doing the exercises in each chapter, you'll have the tools to conquer the fears that may be holding you back and to create a profoundly fulfilling relationship.

It often seems like a relationship is a zero-sum game, where there is only a limited amount of time and energy. A good relationship for most people means having their personal needs met while giving up as little as possible. "If a relationship is not used to meet my needs," you might ask, "won't I have to give up something that I prefer to hold on to?" The real question to ask, however, is, "What if being part of a couple could actually contribute to and expand who I am as an individual?" In an ideal world, a perfect relationship between two perfect individuals would meet all the needs of each partner, with no disagreements. But how can couples ever achieve, let alone sustain, such an idealized state? So far, our experience as marital therapists married to each other for more than three decades has shown us that not many can.

What Is Couple as One?

In this book, we look at couples in a unique way. In our view two people in a relationship create a third entity, what we call "Couple"—not "a couple" or "the couple" or even "our couple," but simply "Couple" with a capital C. Without an article or a possessive adjective in front of it, Couple conveys more a way of being than an object to have or acquire. You might think of Couple as a child that two people nurture together. This third entity is created by contributions from each individual, but it has a life, a being, of its own, with its own characteristics. It can act or behave differently than either of the "parents." It can take on challenges separately and can even support the goals of the "parents" individually. It can do things as a unit that an individual cannot do. You might also think of Couple as you would a business enterprise. A company is made up of separate workers, but the goals to be achieved are the company's. If the company is a success, there is a greater chance that its workers will feel happy and accomplished. If the workers are devoted to the company, the company can function better for the workers.

When two people in a relationship are struggling to change, repair damage or divide up their responsibilities, the entity Couple can come to the rescue. This represents a shift in how most of us think about being in a relationship. It requires working together as a team, with the team's goals in mind, not just the goals of the individuals. The couple that works together as a team has "Couple Power." Couple Power is the combined energy of the twosome directed toward the goals of their couple, or Couple. This entails putting *Couple* first, rather than *me* first. Then the couple is able to produce growth and fulfillment for the individuals.

Consider a couple racing together on a tandem bicycle. Both riders provide energy and commitment to the goal of winning the race. To achieve that end, each has a different contribution to make. The person in front, the pilot, must steer the bicycle, set the speed and look for opportunities to pass other competitors. The role of the person in the rear, the stoker, is to provide as much power as possible for the bike. Each rider is committed to winning the race but provides something unique. Without each person doing what they do best, the team will not succeed. While racing, the riders do not wonder, *Am I doing fifty percent of the work?* They are both giving 100 percent for the victory of the team. The same holds true for couples. When the goal is clear, each person will do what is best for the team, without worrying about how much they are contributing. It is about their commitment to winning. If the team wins, they each win.

Let's look at an example of one couple who embraced the concept of Couple as One after a rough patch in their marriage. Jan and Jim each had careers of their own. Jim was a teacher at the local high school, and Jan worked as a real estate agent. With the birth of their third daughter, their family included three children under the age of seven, and Jan and Jim began to argue about who was doing the most work around the house and with the girls. Jan was nursing their infant daughter and was always tired. She kept asking Jim to pick up the slack around the house. He was already working extra hours as a coach after school to make ends meet. He tried to understand Jan's fatigue and her frustration but really didn't know what more she expected him to do. They both were overworked and at the end of their rope. Jan focused her resentment on Jim, while he blamed Jan for their deteriorating home life.

They began marriage counseling with us and followed our suggestion to take on the increased demands of parenting as a joint project. "The problem is not with either of you," we told them. "It is that you are operating as individuals, without knowing the common goal. Let your couple take it on." We asked them to make a list of what needed to be done every day and to be sure to include some time just for their couple. Jan used a spreadsheet form from her office, and Jim found a program to list the tasks and their schedule whenever they turned their home computer on. They had fun designing the project and including time with each other in the schedule, and so even in the process of organizing, they began working together to solve the challenge of time management. Couple took on the problem, not Jim and Jan separately. They changed the "lens" through which they looked at their couple and stopped blaming each other. The problem was no longer between them; instead, they stood together against the problem.

How does this entity Couple get created? It did take Jim and Jan some time to realize that pulling together, rather than separately, lightened their load. What was necessary to allow them to join forces? First of all, they had to have a *commitment* to work things out—not just a commitment to the other person but a commitment to the relationship. You probably grew up thinking that you needed to find the right *person* to be with, but what is really needed is for two people to form the right *relationship*. The couple needs more care than the individuals. Taking care of the other person may lead to anger and resentment over time, but when both partners take care of the relationship, the relationship will take care of them. When both partners care about and nurture the relationship, Couple becomes the most important focus, not the individuals. The commitment that is needed is staying together as Couple. This commitment does not threaten the personhood of the partners so long as they believe that the relationship will take care of their individual needs. How to establish and maintain such a commitment is the focus of the first part of this book.

If you are committed to your relationship working, then you will tackle difficulties together. If you say, "We are committed to staying in our relationship no matter what for a long, long time, and we need to deal with the daily challenges and annoyances of life," you will then begin to look for ways to cooperate and solve problems together as they arise. Each partner in the relationship will not carry an accumulating load of unexpressed frustration, which is the straw that breaks the back of too many relationships. You won't continually "vote" on whether or not you will stay together. If you know yourself as Couple, because you said so, you *are* Couple, and you stop worrying about what if you were this way or that way. Couple is, then, not a place to get to; it is a place to come from. A powerful couple is created and then sets about living a life together that is profoundly satisfying for both partners. That is the possibility of *lifelong love*.

Why Is Lifelong Love the Exception Rather Than the Rule?

If lifelong love is so appealing, and if living life together as Couple is so satisfying, why are both of these so rare? We have concluded that one of the main reasons for this is the culture we Westerners live in, a culture that in recent decades spawned the "Me Generation," an idea still very much with us. Historian and social critic Christopher Lasch was one of the first to point a finger at pathological narcissism as the cause of a spiritual and relationship crisis in America. In his 1979 book *The Culture of Narcissism: American Life in an Age of Diminishing Expectations,* he writes: "To live for the moment is the prevailing passion—to live for yourself, not for your predecessors or posterity." Of all the challenges to relationships that couples currently face, then, the most significant and pervasive is the prevailing notion of living "for yourself," the notion that being independent and getting your own needs met comprise the highest form of personal functioning. Losing one's autonomy, individuality, and personal power and control is the primary concern in individual-centered relationships. In such relationships, the couple is simply an agreed-upon arrangement between two individuals for the personal fulfillment and pleasure of each.

While there are certainly some positive aspects of individualism, such as increased freedom of expression, too many couples end up being premature and unnecessary casualties of it. Many researchers have noted that the high divorce rate in America seems to be a direct result of our society's emphasis on the individual. In a culture oriented toward the rights of the "rugged individualist," the divorce option is all too attractive, and exercising this option is all too commonplace. It is the only option that makes sense to utilitarian individuals who view a relationship as a nonbinding contract between two consenting adults to meet their respective self-interests. If the relationship no longer meets their needs, the logical solution is to dissolve it. This solution undermines the possibility of forming and maintaining the most basic and elemental of social units and has dire consequences for children, families and society.

As a society, we tend to think that happy people make happy couples. Consider that the reverse, in fact, may be true. It is our experience that happy couples make happy people. The difference is subtle but profound. To enhance lifelong love, you don't necessarily need to "work on yourself"; you need to work on your relationship and your own part in it. In fact, it may be much easier and less threatening to look at your relationship and create a vision for it than to try to keep analyzing yourself.

How to Create Couple as One

If Couple is what generates and protects lifelong love, learning how to create it is essential. It is all about acquiring the skills, behaviors and habit of "we." Is there a "we" in your relationship that is distinct from the two "I's" or individuals? A look at your current attitudes and lifestyle can give you some answers.

Exercise: First Steps to Creating Couple

Together with your partner, answer the following questions. Use this as an opportunity to begin a dialogue about changing the way you view your relationship.

- Do we imagine being married forever? If not, why not?

- Who makes the decisions for our couple? Is this working or not?

- What are the characteristics of our couple when we are together?

- What strengths do we have together that we do not have individually?

- What do we imagine we will be doing twenty-five years from now?

By answering these questions, you will be able to determine whether Couple as One is there for you now and, if it is not, to begin the process of creating it.

From Problem to Possibility:
The Entity Couple Takes Charge

Myra and Dan were at the mall, looking at the window display at Victoria's Secret. Myra said, "What do you think of that?" pointing at a scanty negligee on a very thin mannequin. "For you?

I don't think so," was Dan's reply. It had just slipped out. Still, Myra thought to herself, *I really want to kill him! I could lose a little weight. I know he wants me to, but he does nothing to help. In fact, he just makes these veiled sarcastic remarks. By the way, bucko, you could drop some flab yourself!* She had a fleeting fantasy of making a grand entrance into their TV room, looking sexy and twenty pounds lighter, modeling a new bikini as Dan sat there. Then she fantasized that he would wake up, see her and bolt upright as she walked out the door to meet the handsome twenty-something carpenter who had installed their new kitchen cabinets. She and the carpenter would have a flirtatious drink at a local bar. *It would serve Dan right,* she thought. Then she sighed heavily.

Dan, of course, had his own fantasy. He remembered that trip to the mall, too. Only he had been wondering what that young brunette sales associate at Victoria's Secret would look like in that negligee. At that juncture, he had stopped himself from further daydreaming. *Myra is very attractive, he'd thought, but in the last ten years or so, as the kids have gotten older, she has gotten a bit dowdy. She is not buff or sexy anymore, and she seems to lack the will to do something about it.* He did not want to be critical, but he wished she would take more pride in her appearance.

Dan and Myra's future as a couple was uncertain. Unless something changed, Myra was likely to continue to feel unsupported by and resentful of Dan. This could lead to her becoming angry enough to lose weight to spite him, or she might give up on weight loss and decide that her extra pounds were just something he would have to put up with. And, of course, the worst-case scenario was that Dan's nasty, uncaring remarks would compel her to leave the relationship and seek approval and appreciation elsewhere. Dan, on the other hand, faced the prospect of reconciling himself to the likelihood that Myra was not going to lose weight and might actually gain more. When he imagined all the more attractive alternatives, he felt doomed to a life without real passion.

Before any of these scenarios played out, Dan and Myra began to change the script, to imagine some new possibility and to consider taking on the weight together. One day Dan had a new thought about this issue that was driving a wedge between them! *If I lose a little weight myself, it might encourage her.* He knew that his response to Myra as they gazed at the Victoria's Secret window display had hurt her feelings. He had seen that "you're not attracted to me anymore" look in her eye that day, a look he had noticed more than once. For a moment, as he allowed himself to experience her sadness, he felt his own. Then he sighed heavily and thought, *What if the future is not so predictable and dull? What if Myra were beautiful and sexy again and really attentive? That would be so much easier than sucking it up or starting over in a new relationship.* Myra gained a fresh perspective on the matter while having coffee with a friend one day. She asked herself a few straightforward questions: "What if the future was not so gloomy? What if I had the support I need to become thinner and alluring, and what if Dan became attentive, loving and passionate again?" These revelations laid the groundwork for the creation of Couple, opening up the possibility that Myra and Dan might actually realize their mutual desire for a loving relationship. Later on, in Chapter Four, we describe the creative way in which they accomplished this.

How might you create a new possibility for Couple in your own relationship? We will show you how to begin by sharing your dreams and visions for your couple, while exploring what you think your partner envisions for your relationship. Using the guidelines that we present here, you will come to see that your mutual aspirations as a couple will inspire you to act and create a joint vision for your future together.

To summarize, the first step in creating the entity Couple is making the commitment to being Couple. Remember, this is not a commitment to the other person in the relationship, but to the relationship itself. The partners in a relationship become cocreators of the entity Couple through a process of declaring its existence together. Once this commitment to Couple is established, you can "live from" that vision to address any problems or situations you face. Rather than just reacting individually to your problems, you devise joint strategies and solutions based on your joint commitment to Couple. In other words, the difficulties you face are not the domain of each of you separately; they are the responsibility of the couple and can be solved by being Couple. The power needed to overcome obstacles—and to achieve lifelong love—that "Couple Power" is in the entity you are together.

Let us recall the words of Leonard Cohen at the opening of this chapter, "Dance me to the end of love." Couple, the entity, is indeed like a dance. It is not static but is always moving. The dance is more than just the actions of the individual dancers; it entails one action, a single expression of movement. Each couple has its own unique dance. We can also say that each couple has its own "personality." We often examine how people act when they are with each other, and we evaluate each person's personality. In the process we can see that their couple has a personality as well. Some of these personalities are very common, and as marital therapists, we encounter them all the time. In the next chapter, we look at some of the most common personalities and how they may stand in the way of lifelong love, or how they may empower it.

CHAPTER TWO

Couple Personalities:

The Four Types

*"Emotion, which is suffering, ceases to be suffering
as soon as we form a clear and precise picture of it."*

—Benedict de Spinoza in Victor Frankl's *Man's Search for Meaning*

When thinking about someone, you oftentimes consider what kind of personality s/he has. You may view a certain individual as interesting, unusual, lovable, maybe even repulsive. Personality is a characteristic pattern of behavior that appears over and over again in a variety of life situations. Some people are outgoing, for instance, or quiet or even passive. As with individuals, a number of common patterns of behavior exist for couples. We call these "couple personalities."

Maybe you don't discern a pattern of behavior in your own couple, but it is usually obvious to others. You probably notice this pattern in couples you know. Sometimes you like the two individuals in a couple, but you are put off by how they interact together. Or maybe you even dislike the two people but find their couple personality pleasing. Maybe they are funny or endearing together, or argumentative or unpleasant. Perhaps they are sarcastic or just act silly. Some couples are fun to be with while others are not, and, in the case of the latter, you may find that you would rather spend time with the individual than the couple. You may even say, "She is much more fun when she is not with him."

While each couple has its own particular character, just as individuals do, over decades of working with couples, we have identified three common couple personality types: the Romanticized Couple, the Traditional Couple and the Self-Focused Couple. Like individuals' personalities, there is nothing right or wrong about any of these personality types, but if you get "stuck" in any one particular way of acting or being together, it may cause you to feel restricted, unfulfilled, trapped or even depressed. This is especially true when a couple is dealing with a change in circumstances or conditions. Although the personality traits of couples seem as innate as those of individuals, fortunately, it is possible to modify them with proper guidance and motivation and, in so doing, liberate yourself from those feelings of being restricted or trapped. Having an awareness of your particular couple personality traits is the crucial place to start any "reform." Just being cognizant of your basic tendencies gives you more control and choice about them. The important thing at this point is to be open to examining your couple personality together until, as Spinoza says, "we form a clear and precise picture of it."

As you read through the descriptions of the three common couple personality types, you may notice that one of them fits your own relationship. It may be upsetting to see yourself in one of the types, but remember that change is possible, and you can recast and reconfigure your couple personality at any time.

The Romanticized Couple

Charles and Sally had dated for over a year when they decided to get engaged. They were incredibly drawn to each other and couldn't be together enough. They made love, deeply and passionately, almost every night, often into the early morning hours. They were so absorbed in each other, it was like there was no outside world sometimes. Eventually the late nights started to wear them out. Charles got so run-down that he developed walking pneumonia; Sally missed a lot of days at work and was reprimanded by her boss. She was concerned about her work-life balance, but she and Charles were in love. Their friends gave up trying to spend any time with them, because they seemed interested only in each other.

After they got married, something changed between them. They couldn't seem to sustain the passion they had for each other before they started living together. They had other things to do together, like keeping their apartment clean and the refrigerator full, and looking after their new cat, Fritz. When they were trading off days at each other's house during their courtship, they didn't have shared responsibilities; it was just about being in love. As a married couple, they felt more distant. They couldn't have sex all the time, but they were stuck in the belief that sex was the only way to express their love for each other. They started fighting about little things more and more.

On their second anniversary, they went to a very nice restaurant for a special dinner. They enjoyed each other's company, but by now the excitement was gone from their relationship. Over dinner Charles noticed that Sally seemed a bit bored and was staring off into space. Meanwhile he was flirting with the beautiful young waitress who served them. They joked about how long two years seemed to them and what it might have been like if they had not gotten together. They laughed, but both were secretly wondering if it was time to find a new partner. Charles leaned over and kissed Sally over a glass of wine, but the kiss was not passionate, just warm and familiar. There was no sense of being carefree and spontaneous, as they had been before. Now they experienced boredom with one another and felt that their relationship was stale and predictable. Before, they were tired out from all the passion; now the romance had faded and their relationship was tiresome.

Charles and Sally had fallen into a fixed pattern of relating to each other. It had taken them over and had not left any space to grow, especially once they started living together. They couldn't see past their romantic ideals to create what might be next for them, individually or as a couple. They had become rigid and inflexible in their expectations. For example, if Charles didn't bring home flowers every week, Sally felt disappointed. If they didn't have sex at least every other day, one or both of them became angry and distant. They thought there was something wrong if they had a simultaneous climax only half the time they made love. If they didn't have something special planned to do together every weekend, they got upset—especially if one of them had made plans to do something without the other or there was work to do around the apartment. Their couple had developed a personality that no longer worked for them.

Sally and Charles are a Romanticized Couple. At the pinnacle of their romance, the partners in a Romanticized Couple are "in love" and are deeply absorbed in each other, to the near exclusion of the outside world. When at work, they want to be at home with each other; when separated, they want to be together. They spend a lot of time telephoning, emailing or texting each other when they are apart, and they devote many hours to daydreaming about what they will do as soon as they are together again.

Remember Shakespeare's *Romeo and Juliet?* Blinded by their love and passion, the young lovers become impatient and reckless, which leads to their tragic end. Romeo and Juliet's relationship is all about being together at all costs, despite the risks they face. They become caught up in the moment, so much so that when Romeo believes his beloved is dead, he kills himself without considering other options or checking carefully to make sure he knows all the facts about the situation. He is not creative or flexible in the face of adversity. Juliet acts out of the same passion. Both expect that love will conquer all. It is their impulsivity and inflexibility, a result of their blinding love, that does them in. Romanticized love is blind, indeed.

Perhaps more than the other couple personality types, Romanticized Couples—like Romeo and Juliet, or Charles and Sally—often fall victim to the idealized images and notions of love and romance permeating our culture. We describe in the next chapter how television, film, radio, music and print media all glorify the romantic relationship, generating unrealistic expectations and unreachable goals for couples—and unremitting pressures, especially on the Romanticized Couple. When these expectations and goals are not met, and the pressures are too great, partners that see no other options will often feel despair and may even decide to end the relationship and look for one that better meets their needs. A critical moment for Romanticized Couples is when the highly romantic stage of a relationship, what we might call infatuation, fades. Research shows that this stage typically lasts only twelve to eighteen months or so. Then the hormones and biochemicals that were activated in the body by the state of infatuation start to vanish, and the couple must adjust. Romanticized Couples, like many celebrity couples, whose relationships are so often romanticized by the media, often encounter difficulty adjusting to the end of the infatuation stage. Other personality types, like the next two described below, may have no difficulty making this adjustment and may go on for years without encountering a bump in the road, though not necessarily with any true sense of satisfaction or fulfillment.

The Traditional Couple

The life of a Romanticized Couple is wonderful and enlivening while in its heyday. Some couples begin as Romanticized Couples and then move on to another couple type, such as the Traditional Couple. Others may never experience a romanticized or erotic phase at all and start out as a Traditional Couple. Love needs to be part of any relationship, but a particular sort of love and caring characterizes this second common couple personality type. Partners in a Traditional Couple often describe themselves as loving but not necessarily "in love" in a romantic way. Consider the following:

Mildred and Richard had been married for nearly forty years. They had dated in college and then got married. During the course of their marriage, he worked constantly and steadily climbed the corporate ladder, first securing a place in middle management, then becoming the CEO of a small company and then, finally, emerging as the leader of a large corporation. All this time Mildred minded the home fires, raising their three daughters, cooking, keeping an impeccable household and being the "hostess with the mostest." Richard was very happy. He loved Mildred and appreciated her support. Mildred, however, was not so satisfied. She had been afraid to tell Richard, but for years she had been angry that once the girls were in school full-time, she did not go back to work. She had gotten a degree in social work and had always wanted to practice her trade, but Richard had insisted from the beginning that she stay home with the kids. She had agreed that this was important and that she would do this for a while. Finally, it came time to consider retirement. The girls were grown and had their own families, and Richard would soon leave the company he had worked at for so many years. It was Mildred who requested that they go to see a counselor. Richard was a bit confused about why counseling was necessary, but he assumed it had to do with the prospect of his being home more after retirement, and he recognized that maybe they needed to communicate a bit better.

At the first session, Peter asked each of them to describe their relationship. Richard began by describing them as a happy couple blessed with wonderful children and a lifetime filled with marvelous memories, fun vacations, and great love and satisfaction. Much to Richard's surprise, Mildred told a very different story. Through tears and small sobs, she recounted a life of struggle, frustration, anger and hurt. He had never really listened to her concerns or thought of her well-being, she said, and he was absent much of the time and was never really there for her or their daughters. She had wanted a career of her own and a chance to feel like a professional, not just a mom, but there was no time or space for that. "Richard's career took precedence all the time," she complained. She felt trapped in her lifestyle, and now that the children were grown, and he was ready to retire, she saw a chance for some freedom. "Now it's finally my turn," she said. "I want to do what I want to do, or I'm going to leave." Richard was shocked, but he loved his wife, and he didn't want their relationship to end. They both realized they had to make some changes in their couple if they wanted it to work for both of them.

Mildred and Richard were clearly stuck in the Traditional Couple personality. This way of being as a couple is marked by rigid role expectations for each member. The roles are defined by outside forces, such as culture, or by values learned or internalized while growing up and observing role models. In couples of this personality type, one partner, especially the female partner, or even both partners often feel unheard, taken for granted or unfulfilled. Traditional Couples usually appear to others to be quite functional and happy. Things get done, and the partners seem to know what it is that they are supposed to be doing. They may even feel gratified by what they accomplish for a while. As time goes on, however, conforming to role expectations becomes a drag on life satisfaction for both partners, and expectations need to change for the couple to grow and for each partner to be fulfilled. Traditional Couples that do not become more flexible with the passage of time, like Richard and Mildred, are the ones most likely to experience feelings of boredom and dissatisfaction and to endure marital turmoil.

The Self-Focused Couple

The third common couple personality type is the Self-Focused Couple. In Self-Focused Couples the partners center their attention on their individual concerns and primarily function independently of each other. While the partners may receive some support from each other, they generally have separate careers and agendas. They do not feel connected or interdependent. Rather, the couple is made up of two self-contained individuals, with their own goals and desires, operating separately from each other in the outside world. The couple may form an alliance or a relationship to support or even coach one another, but ultimately their intense individuality, as we discussed before, stands in the way of their operating as a team and being flexible and fulfilled as a couple. In short, many Self-Focused Couples do not operate as Couple.

Cal and Judy met after each had been working for a number of years. He was a dentist, and she was a high school teacher. After they got married, they each continued in their careers. Judy's school and Cal's practice were nearly ninety minutes apart by car. They decided to live someplace midway between her school and his office. They both had to commute, Judy had papers to grade and Cal had a practice to build, so they spent a lot of time apart. When they were together, they would talk about their work and get advice from each other. Over time they both became very successful. Both Cal and Judy loved their work, and a measure of their success was that they became busier and busier. Cal began to attend dental conferences a few times a year. Judy worked with the teachers in her district and also developed a career working with the local union. They were proud of each other and loved each other, but they just weren't together very much. When they did spend time together, they had many chores to tackle, such as fixing up the house and getting their taxes in on time. They began to argue a lot about little things, and that made it even less fun for them to be together.

About this time, Cal hired a new receptionist in his office. She was young and beautiful, and he became attracted to her. When he was at work, he didn't have to deal with all the things he had to confront at home. He could flirt with the receptionist, take her to lunch and not have to listen to complaints about projects left undone or about spending too much time at the office. No nagging and no complaints.

When Cal and Judy were together, they sensed a distance and wariness between them, which neither of them liked. They felt good about their jobs, but they didn't feel like they were lovers at all, just partners or maybe even roommates. While each of them wanted to have more time to spend together doing fun things and hanging out, neither of them really wanted to jeopardize their careers. They were leading separate lives as a Self-Focused Couple, and they didn't feel the way they used to about each other. Eventually, Cal had an affair with his receptionist and another woman as well. Cal and Judy dealt with this in therapy, as described in Chapter Eight.

Self-Focused Couples are highly visible. They are everywhere. This includes many celebrity couples. Such couples often encounter difficulty in their marriage because there is rarely room in the Self-Focused Couple for two stars at the same time. Certainly, everyone has a right to their place in the sun, but often stardom becomes an obsession for the star, too, in an individualistic culture that seems to worship celebrities. With a few notable exceptions, celebrity couples gain attention owing to their personal achievements rather than the quality of their "coupleness." Also, celebrities are frequently under the spotlight, and finding time to be together as a couple is not easy. With the exception of their beautiful homes and adorable children, the mainstream media has very little interest in how famous couples work out the daily routines of being together.

Variety Is the Spice of Life

Many of the characteristics of each of the common couple personality types described here are important and even essential for couples to be happy and stable at different times in their lives and in different situations. Aspects of each of these couple personality types would be helpful to most couples at some point. The behaviors of the Romanticized Couple personality, for instance, may be crucial for falling in love and for special occasions. Similarly, the Traditional Couple's penchant for defining roles is essential for effective functioning and communication in a couple. And the Self-Focused Couple's inclination for establishing independence and autonomy is vital to the healthy maintenance of individuals and Couple as One.

Problems occur when you get stuck in any one of these personality patterns for a long period of time, are unable to see or pursue other options when needed for the good of your couple and are not happy or comfortable any other way. For example, if Romanticized Couples stay in the "gaga" stage for too long, they lose sight of the bigger picture. Without a sense of choice, variety and flexibility in a relationship, the development of Couple as One essentially stops and may even disappear. Human beings are creatures of habit, and those habits can be hard to break. We get caught up in repeating patterns or roles, like those of breadwinner, helpmate or lover, and we search for a partner who will play the complementary or opposite roles. Conflict inevitably arises when we do not get what we expected, or when we thought we wanted one thing, only to discover that what we really wanted was something else.

Sometimes, especially if you are in a Romanticized or Traditional relationship, you may want your partner to take a caretaker role, but when s/he does, you often end up feeling controlled or powerless. The expectations are usually unrealistic from the beginning and generally lead to disappointment, resignation or sometimes even the ending of the relationship. When you stay together, if the relationship does not develop and grow, you are likely to experience decreasing levels of satisfaction.

The sad truth is that the research shows that the longer a couple is married, the less likely they are to divorce *but* the less likely they are to report being content in their marriage. Many couples have satisfying relationships over the long haul. Unfortunately, however, for many couples, what may appear from the outside to be a "mature" marriage may simply be a union of two people who have settled into a pattern and expect less from their relationship. It's kind of like a piece of fruit that has been sitting on the counter for too long: you might assume it has ripened, when in fact it just smells bad!

Traditional Couples are usually very efficient in accomplishing the tasks required of parents and working families, or dealing with an ill or disabled family member, or managing an aging relative in the home. When stuck in the role-defined behaviors for too long, however, one or both partners often feel stifled or used. Taking on specific roles in your couple is empowering; however, knowing when to alter those roles is essential. If you fulfill the same roles for too long, you will likely end up feeling bored or even exploited. Self-Focused Couples engage in some very useful behaviors, too. Separate interests and careers typically give rise to a sense of satisfaction and self-fulfillment. When such separate activities are pursued at the expense of spending loving and caring time together, however, the partners in a Self-Focused Couple, like Cal and Judy, lose the experience of themselves as Couple.

Fortunately, there is a viable alternative to letting your relationship become rigid, stagnant or immobilized. We call this alternative the "Dynamic Couple." This type of couple is perhaps less familiar than the three distinct couple personalities just described, but it is more likely to succeed over the long haul. It incorporates the essential qualities of all three couple personality types and includes a flexible approach that allows for creative ways of relating at different times. This ability to be flexible and to create things together in a variety of situations, that is, to be "cocreating," makes a couple dynamic and alive over time. We say "cocreating" rather than "cocreative" because creating is an ongoing process, not a static characteristic. The act of creating together becomes part of the life that the Dynamic Couple shares together.

The Dynamic Couple

There is no right or wrong way to be a Dynamic Couple. What makes Dynamic Couples successful is discovering what is most satisfying for them as an entity at any moment in their lives and committing to that as a team. This kind of couple exhibits lifelong love in its purest form. However, you may not recognize the Dynamic Couples who cross your path, as you rarely see them. There seem to be few positive role models, few examples of this way of being a couple around today. Unlike some Eastern and African cultures, Western culture seems more accustomed to change than to long-term intimate commitment.

The media is not much help when it comes to providing positive expectations and role models for lifelong love. We read articles in *USA Today* and other publications describing famous couples who are divorcing or who *as yet* have no plans to divorce. Negativity sells, but it also inflicts damage. Perhaps most important, it keeps us from noticing the celebrity couples whose relationships actually work beautifully, though they seem to be few and far between. Those famous couples, and other couples described below, are excellent examples of Dynamic Couples, and their characteristics are worthy of our attention.

Patricia, an interior designer, and her husband, Josh, an architect, thrived on having fun, traveling and going to the movies and the theater together. But when their daughter was born, everything seemed to change. Patricia was less available, and Josh threw himself into his work. She became dissatisfied with his parenting, and he felt he was not getting enough companionship from her. By working together, they began to see parenting and being part of a couple as a joint "building project," like a house they might work on together, with Josh doing the architectural drawings and Patricia designing the interior. Each had a significant role to play in the project that was their relationship, with cooperation and clear communication as essential components. As a result, they began to schedule time alone together and as a whole family on a regular basis, literally designing the time they wanted to spend with their daughter and with each other.

A married couple with different circumstances, Ivan and Barbara, provide another example of the cocreating process. Ivan took on a new job working the early shift at a factory in a neighboring town, which meant a commute that began at 5:00 a.m. His wife, Barbara, a homemaker and an author, was most inspired to write in the late-night hours. Faced with a scheduling challenge, Ivan and Barbara kept looking at the situation until they created something that worked for each of them individually as well as a couple: Barbara would awaken in mid-afternoon and would prepare a dinner to share with Ivan once he arrived home. Then, after he went to bed, she would spend several hours writing in solitude. Before she went to sleep, she would prepare breakfast for Ivan and then would see him off to work. Though it may seem old-fashioned or role constricting to some, this arrangement functioned very well for both partners, and their relationship has remained effective and fulfilling for over fifty years.

The unique schedule that worked for Ivan and Barbara might not work for other couples. What is worth noting about both these couples is their commitment to working together cooperatively as a united team to solve difficult problems in their relationship. Rather than thinking only of their own needs or sacrificing to "make it work," they kept going until they created something powerful that worked for them as individuals and as a couple. They were flexible and did not get stuck in their old patterns with the advent of new circumstances, such as a new baby or a new job. They were able to see these new circumstances as dynamic opportunities for creating something new. They did not look for someone else to tell them the "right way" to work it out, as there was no "right answer" to be found.

The most important thing is finding out what is most workable and satisfying for your couple at any particular moment in your lives. The first "particular moment" usually arrives at the very beginning of working out a relationship. Even with the romance that accompanies falling in love, cocreating is required from the outset to keep the love light shining for a lifetime.

The kind of commitment that characterizes the Dynamic Couple is distinct from what happens with the other three couple personality types. Instead of being dependent upon your partner for your happiness, you are committed to working together to meet the common goals of your couple as a path to joint happiness. Thus, as in the examples above, rather than getting consumed with doubts about being sufficiently in love with each other, the focus is on creating ways to foster the commitment to your couple vision. The goal of the Dynamic Couple is not to remain together no matter what the cost; that would be the kind of codependency that often characterizes both Romanticized and Traditional Couples. The intention of the Dynamic Couple is also not to create a rigid system, which may lead both partners—especially if the couple is the Self-Focused type—to feel trapped.

Rather, the Dynamic Couple's goal is to create inspiration and security for maintaining lifelong love.

The way that Dynamic Couples communicate is also distinct from that of the other couple personality types. Dynamic Couples engage in what we call "responsible speaking and listening." It involves examining your own part in any interaction, as well as respecting and honoring your partner's thoughts and feelings. Take, for example, Lannie and Becca, who had been engaged for more than three years. He was Catholic and she was Jewish. Some of the delay in scheduling their marriage was a result of the disagreements they had every time they started to plan their wedding ceremony. With the help of some friends who had been in a similar situation, they each took time just to listen to the other's concerns and desires and to spell out how they might design the ceremony. Each was able to listen without injecting his or her own concerns until it was the other's turn to speak. To their surprise, they found there was little difference in what they wanted, and they actually invented some new things together that neither of them had considered before. The ceremony became "theirs," not his or hers.

The hallmark of this kind of communication in Dynamic Couples is thinking outside the box. Rather than relying on a fixed way of doing things, as is characteristic of the other couple personalities, Dynamic Couples are willing to entertain solutions they had never thought of or tried before. The Traditional Couple may stick with their defined roles of homemaker and breadwinner, for example, even if they are miserable, because they are too restricted or afraid to try anything new, like switching roles if that might help them. A Dynamic Couple, on the other hand, designs something unique, such as Ivan and Barbara did in the example above, to create a new way to achieve a goal that is satisfactory to both partners.

A focus on quality rather than quantity is another characteristic of Dynamic Couples. They value their time together and commit to having it and making it productive and enjoyable. Unlike Romanticized Couples, they do not become so absorbed that they spend countless hours together and eventually become annoyed or bored by the very things they were initially attracted to in each other. In Dynamic Couples, both partners have their own life and personal activities, but unlike Traditional or Self-Focused Couples, they are willing to make a commitment to their relationship itself. They keep the sense of connection and support of their couple with them at all times, even if they are not physically together.

This is what Robert and Laura did when she wanted to go to graduate school across the country, and Robert didn't want to leave their home and his job. After facing the prospect of ending their relationship, they realized they had something stronger than their home and jobs to hold them together, and that was the quality of their commitment to their couple. They then worked out a solution that enabled them to support each other in both of their pursuits and still be together. We will talk about how they did this in more detail in Chapter Five.

Another defining characteristic of Dynamic Couples is that they have a community of other couples that they are connected with in meaningful ways in their lives. While they know that two heads are better than one, they also know that two or more couples are better than one. When the going gets rough, they don't rely only on each other; they are willing to reach out to other couples for support. As mentioned earlier, Romanticized Couples tend to isolate themselves from other couples, eventually leading to more tension or boredom than the partners are able to manage on their own. Without outside support and stimulation, your couple may burn out or slowly lose its vitality.

Traditional and Self-Focused Couples often get support for their individual goals but not their joint goals, which may eventually create more distance between them as they pursue their own interests. We have all witnessed those scenes at a party where the women are in one room, complaining about their husbands, and the men are in another room, getting support for what's wrong with their wives. With those kinds of friends, who needs enemies? Rather, what we need to keep us powerfully creating and sustaining our relationships are friends who value us as a couple.

That is what Natalie and Bruce, who had been married for nearly fifty years, found when they realized that they had many friends and an active social life, but that they were not getting what they needed to become more intimate with each other or with mutual friends. While they loved each other, they began to accept the status quo and realized that some potential was not being fulfilled in their relationship. Both of them began lapsing into sadness. About this time, they moved into a new apartment complex and joined an adult education group there. The chance to share in open dialogue with this new group became the pivotal point where their relationship deepened. "What made the real difference," Natalie said, "was having some of the new couples question why we did certain things and how we came to hold certain beliefs. This opened the opportunity for us to view things from different perspectives. It was like the excitement of being newly married again. Our understanding and caring were profoundly enhanced by being part of a community of couples." They began to share more openly with each other, their friends and families, and they got in touch with a new richness in their own relationship and their relationships with others. There was a noticeable reawakening of their physical intimacy as well.

The Dynamic Couple operates as a joint force or entity that allows both partners to resolve the problems of life together in an interdependent way. This way of being provides freedom from feeling forced to focus on always meeting your own needs and protecting your independence, and it frees up the creative energy that fuels Couple Power and lifelong love. Together the Dynamic Couple generates more force, more energy, more love and more personal satisfaction than the two individuals alone.

To have love that lasts a lifetime, you first need to know what you already have and where you are in the present moment. Working on your relationship without a strong commitment and a clear path may lead to confusion and tension. It would be like going into the wilderness with no map and no sense of direction. You are bound to get lost. So it is important to know where your couple is starting from before venturing into the intimate experience of working on the tasks of Couple Power.

The Couple Personality exercise below will enable you to identify your own couple's predominant pattern based on a list of personality traits of the three common couple personality types. Determine which pattern most accurately describes your couple at the moment. This will give you a place to start from as you continue along the path of lifelong love. Every couple has some of these characteristics. Pick the personality type that fits your couple best. The common couple personality characteristics listed here will help you in completing the exercise.

Common Couple Personality Characteristics

Romanticized Couples

- Spend most or all of their free time with each other
- Spend little time with friends
- Experience being in love all the time
- Are tired much of the time
- Have difficulty concentrating on work or school or other commitments
- Think of each other almost all the time when apart
- Are jealous of their partner's time with others
- Hold an idealized image of their partner
- Have sex or think about sex with their partner frequently
- Feel empty or unhappy when apart, even briefly
- Experience an intense and constant physical attraction

Traditional Couples

- Keep fixed agreements about responsibilities and tasks
- Adhere to traditional values
- One partner often feels taken for granted
- Do the same kind of activities with each other over and over
- One or both partners feel in a "rut"
- Have poor communication regarding upsets or conflicts
- One or both partners are passive in resolving conflicts or making decisions
- Are overly dependent upon the opinions or actions of their partner

Self-Focused Couples

- Spend little time with each other
- Focus on chores, projects, parenting, etc., when together
- Spend a lot of time individually at work or on hobbies
- Talk about work constantly
- Are supportive of their partner's goals
- Focus primarily on individual goals and achievements
- Are often jealous of their partner's success
- Are competitive with their partner
- Have few common leisure or fun activities
- Take separate vacations
- Have few friends or couple friends in common
- Are very busy all the time

Exercise: Identifying Your Couple Personality

Set aside at least a half an hour to work on this exercise with your partner.

THINK: Think about which of the common couple personality characteristics seem to fit your couple at the current time.

DO: Make a list of the couple personality characteristics that fit your couple best. Choose from those listed above and add some of your own. Next, make a list of the Dynamic Couple characteristics that you want to start incorporating into your interactions and daily routines. Finally, list some joint projects that you might work on together in the near future. Note when you plan to start and finish them.

SHARE: What might it be like for you and your partner to have a different couple personality or combination of personalities?

What are your strengths as a couple?

What characteristics of the Dynamic Couple do you already have?

II

Creating Lifelong Love: Building Couple Power with the Four C's

CHAPTER THREE

Commitment:

The First Step toward Lifelong Love

"True love is like a ghost; everybody talks about it, but few have seen it."

—François de La Rochefoucauld,
Reflections, or Sentences and Moral Maxims

Now that you know what a Dynamic Couple is, the next step is to show you how to become one. The key to creating and maintaining this kind of rewarding relationship is what we call the Four C's of Couple Power: commitment, cooperation, communication and community. This chapter explores the first C, commitment, and provides you with several simple—though not simplistic—exercises to complete that are geared toward strengthening your commitment to your relationship. While these tasks are easy to follow, the principles behind them are profound in nature.

The first C, commitment, is the cornerstone of any successful relationship. Without that secure foundation, nothing else really works. You may fall in love, but you don't "fall into" commitment. Of course, love is an important part of the equation, which is why we call this book *Lifelong Love* and not *Lifelong Partnership* or *Lifelong Friendship*. But the intensely romantic part of love lasts only about twelve to eighteen months. Then what? Furthermore, some very viable relationships, like the arranged marriages prevalent in certain cultures, don't start with love; the relationship generally develops into a loving one over time. So while love is necessary, it is usually not enough to maintain a profoundly fulfilling relationship. Something more is needed from each partner to keep their relationship alive and well, and the first ingredient of the something more is *commitment*. Many people are afraid of commitment and have difficulty understanding and dealing with it in their close relationships. The very word may bring up negative associations. The story of the beginning of our own relationship is a case in point.

We met and fell in love while working in the same city, but we soon faced the possibility of being separated by new job opportunities. Phyllis explained, "Peter was offered a job on the East Coast, which was the best position he received, and he asked me to come with him. I felt I could do so only if I also had a job there that I liked. When I did find a good job in the same city, I realized I still had mixed feelings about the whole thing. I had doubts about Peter's commitment to our relationship, and I didn't want to move if we weren't going to get married soon. My biological clock was ticking loudly. While I was in the process of making a decision, Peter and I had several discussions about it. Looking back on it, I realize we invented a creative solution to the issue of our commitment to the relationship. We agreed that we were both serious about our relationship, and that we would make a definite decision about marriage within the year. I came to see that this could be an "adventure" for me, making it more exciting than risky. I also saw that committing to the possibility of our relationship was more important than where I was going to live for the next year."

Peter added, "We saw that we could make a commitment to deciding, rather than a commitment to a particular decision. I knew that having Phyllis come with me might limit other relationship possibilities in my new environment. It would have been safer to move and possibly invite her to join me later. However, it occurred to us that the prospect of exploring our relationship together would be more exciting than doing it separately. Our recent training and work with couples showed us the power of thinking as a couple rather than as individuals and of putting value on our relationship itself. This allowed us to move together to a new place without a sense that one of us was making a sacrifice for the other. Instead, this was something we were committed to doing together for a specific amount of time to find out more about our relationship. And, of course, it worked. A year later, on April 1, I proposed, and we decided to get married. We were both clear that this was not an April fool's joke!" Phyllis's mother, however, remained skeptical about that up until the day of the wedding ceremony!

In retrospect, one of the things that enabled us to choose to stay together was not thinking that we were committing to *each other*. In fact, we barely knew each other, having dated only a few months when we faced the decision about moving. Rather, we were both clear that we were committing to work on a joint vision for our relationship as it was in the moment. We stuck to that agreement, not because we felt we had to, but because we both sincerely felt the desire to work on the possibility of a long-term relationship together. It was clearly a matter of choice on both of our parts.

Every choice of something involves a rejection or loss of something else, so there was also some sadness about what we were not choosing. Phyllis was tired of dating and was looking to settle down. Peter was ready to move on from living life alone and searching for a mate. But both of us regretted leaving our friends and the beautiful California life we had come to know and love. We supported each other in dealing with that loss by sharing our feelings and our ideas about how we could go back and visit—which we have done several times since then.

Of course, this was just the initial step of our commitment. Difficult as it is to decide to move together, it is a whole other thing, you might be thinking, to decide to get married. And you're right. Many couples who move to the same city or even into the same house together never take that step. Research shows, in fact, that contrary to common beliefs, cohabiting couples actually have less chance of lifelong love than couples who do not live together before marriage. We will describe shortly how we came to take the next step, committing to get married, but first let's explore what commitment means.

Commitment to Your Couple

As we discussed in the last chapter, the kind of commitment that characterizes the Dynamic Couple personality is distinct from what happens with the other three couple personality types—it is a shared commitment to what is possible for the couple as an entity. We were able to make a strong commitment to our relationship by focusing on what we were creating together, not what we had hoped for from the other person. This is an active process of *doing* something, not just wishing for the right thing or the right person to show up.

Instead of being dependent upon the other person for their happiness, the partners of a Dynamic Couple focus on working together to meet the common goals of their couple as a path to their joint happiness. Rather than getting stuck in hopes and doubts about being sufficiently in love with each other, they focus on creating specific ways to foster commitment through *dedication* to the couple as an entity. This kind of dedication takes you beyond hoping for a great relationship and gets you into taking actions that will create it. Dedication, in this sense, is not the blind devotion of the Romanticized Couple, which can lead to a tragic ending, like the one Romeo and Juliet endured. Rather, it is what the dictionary defines as "giving wholly or earnestly up to." "Giving up" here means letting go of something freely, not sacrificing or even compromising. As this definition of *dedication* suggests, it entails a complete and purposeful choice—which is romantic in its own way.

The kind of dedicated commitment we are talking about here is also different than *obligation*, which is committing to some person or behavior out of a sense of duty or necessity. Committing to a relationship out of obligation may carry you over some of the rough spots along the way, but it will not support the fulfilling relationship you both want over time. Obligation takes away the sense of freedom of choice so vital to lifelong love. The type of commitment based on obligation is preached in some religious teachings, and couples often end up feeling that they need to stay together out of moral duty. At times that approach may work, but as a long-term solution, it is bound to lead to feelings of resentment or despair.

We probably all know couples who seem like they are struggling or even suffering through their relationship and are experiencing pain or boredom. That is definitely not what we mean by commitment here. The goal of the Dynamic Couple is not to stay together no matter what the cost. Sometimes the cost is emotional or even physical abuse. Commitment can't exist when threats and fear are present. Any kind of abuse is destructive to a relationship and needs to be handled quickly and decisively. It doesn't necessarily mean the end of the relationship, but professional help is usually indicated, as we will discuss in Chapter Eight.

Neither does commitment mean creating a rigid agreement on how the couple will operate, which may result in the couple feeling trapped or limited. This may be perhaps the most negative connotation of commitment. Self-Focused Couples are particularly prone to the fear of being "stuck" in a relationship. They are caught in the dilemma of wanting to have a lifelong relationship but also believing that happiness can be attained only through self-gratification and individual achievement. This kind of self-indulgence puts stress on the relationship, and all too often the partners find escape in separation or even divorce. A destructive pattern of serial marriages or partnerships may follow, with the individual starting relationships over and over without ever really knowing how to commit creatively or powerfully. This kind of person may be termed *commitment avoidant*, driven away from what s/he might really want by an irrational fear of committing. Dynamic Couples, on the other hand, by being *commitment focused*, are able to stay connected to their partner and their relationship while still maintaining a sense of freedom and flexibility. That sense of freedom within a relationship requires a great deal of trust.

We had that kind of trust in the level of our commitment to work together "wholly and earnestly" on our relationship after we moved to the same city together. This process required a good deal of perseverance and patience on both our parts, but we both knew how much was at stake and what our relationship meant to us. It is often at the beginning of relationships when this dilemma of commitment first surfaces. Dating, hanging out, falling in love and even having sex are not nearly as challenging as making a clear choice about what long-term commitment to a relationship means to both partners.

David and Leslie confronted this choice shortly after they got engaged while in graduate school. When it came time for them to apply for professional internships in their field, they had to decide whether to consider only training settings in the same city, which would restrict both their options, or to seek separately the best placements they could get, even though they knew they risked being separated for as long as a year. They both decided that they could trust their relationship enough to work it out no matter what happened, so they chose to apply separately for the best placements. Though they applied for many internships in the same geographic areas, as luck would have it, they ended up at opposite ends of the country. While disappointed, of course, they began planning how they could support each other and meet their individual needs while maintaining their couple commitments. They immediately started saving money for airfare and earmarked accumulated frequent flyer points for trips to visit each other. Leslie was able to live with their best friends, who were newly-weds, and David got help from his sister, who lived near his new workplace. These arrangements helped them to get through the year and to have fun in the process.

Many people, including some professional therapists, believe that a person needs to be emotionally strong and healthy as an individual before s/he can be part of a healthy relationship. It may be surprising to you that we have actually found that the situation can be the reverse. The commitment to the relationship helps create and support the healthy individual. The sense of security and support that comes with being part of a committed relationship makes individuals feel safe, bolstering emotional health. In other words, it's not just healthy people that make healthy relationships; healthy relationships can make healthy people. In the last chapter we talk much more about this concept and give several examples of it.

Creating a Couple Vision

Do you have a vision for your relationship? One dictionary definition of *vision* is "the ability to imagine and prepare for the future," and this is what we have in mind. Research shows that people who create specific visions for the future are more likely to fulfill them. Many people have written and spoken about the value of creating visions. Marriage researcher Scott Stanley defines a vision as "an image or ideal that guides people, often providing meaning, motivation, and inspiration for the tasks ahead" (Stanley 2005, 170). The vision for a relationship often takes the form of a shared metaphor or statement that the couple designs with language that is meaningful and unique to them. A busy dual-career couple we know shared with us a wonderful example of this. They repeat this statement when alone or together as they ponder their loving but often long-distance relationship: "We travel through life together, staying in the same internal place of our couple; we know, then, there's no other place—the best place."

Many famous people in history created visions that inspired whole nations and the world—for good or for ill. Consider the Reverend Martin Luther King, Jr., and his "I Have a Dream" speech. His vision of social justice and economic freedom for all, encapsulated in that speech, touched the hearts of people all around the world. It served then, and still serves, to uplift people confronting obstacles on the path to realizing that dream. And in 1961, before a special joint session of Congress, President John F. Kennedy created a vision of the future when he announced that the United States would land a man safely on the moon by the end of the decade. No one knew then exactly how that could be done. The effect of Kennedy's vision, however, was to cause people to see the future differently and to begin making plans to realize that destiny. New resources were generated and new technology was invented, all to bring this vision into being.

Similarly, the job of a Dynamic Couple is to envision the higher purpose of the relationship, one that has room to grow and constantly re-create itself. Individual goals and perspectives are shared not to bolster the partners but to contribute to a mutual view of what will support and nurture the relationship. This sharing requires going beyond your individual wants and needs to help develop a joint vision that integrates your separate perspectives. The integrated vision then works to support each individual's needs and goals. Neither of you has to give up your own vision. On the contrary, Couple becomes an avenue for enhancing your individual pursuits. Creating a joint vision, then, becomes an opportunity for each of you to see and reinforce the best in each other.

So how do you create a couple vision? Some of us have positive role models from our past to emulate, such as the relationships of our parents and grandparents. For others, the past is filled with negative models, which we want to avoid. Some of us had parents who lived lives of quiet desperation for the kids' sake or went through a bitter divorce. The popular media, which seems obsessed with celebrity divorces or royal marriages, doesn't provide many positive or realistic role models either. No wonder, then, that most people are frightened by the idea of commitment and have difficulty creating believable possibilities for a relationship. Rather than imagining what is possible, they end up creating visions based on what is missing and trying to "fix" it. This fear makes it very difficult for a couple to grasp the higher purpose of the relationship. Creating a couple vision might entail letting go of some of your fear of commitment.

Creating a couple vision does not entail inventing a set of behaviors to adhere to or coming up with a list of things to *do;* it involves designing new ways of *being* for your couple to "live into" for the future. Even thinking about creating a vision may be a challenge for those of us who grew up in a culture that puts the material and the concrete over the spiritual and the mysterious. However, it is possible to come up with a vision that is inspiring for both partners in your couple, even without having role models to rely on. Here are some ways to accomplish that.

Sharing life histories

Looking back on the process of committing to our own relationship, we realized that what sustained us in our decision-making process about getting married was the vision we created while we were driving across country together to move to our new home. First, we told each other our individual life histories, focusing particularly on past relationships. This was eye-opening to us individually and as a couple, and it prompted us to envision a new future together. We imagined ourselves as a vibrant, happy and successful couple. We were then able to talk excitedly about having children, being in careers where we could do some work together and owning a house on the water. (The house on the water took the longest to materialize!)

Exercise: Sharing Your Life Histories

Take some time and share your life histories with each other, focusing on the relationships you had in the past. Interrupt each other only to ask for clarification. Do not try to evaluate or analyze each other's stories.

Sharing dreams

Sharing your life histories is a way to remember and acknowledge the past. Sharing your dreams is a way to imagine the present and wonder about the future. The idea is not to use your dreams to try and fix or re-create the past, but to invent a whole new idea about the future. The dreams you share may be daydreams, night dreams or what we call "visioning dreams." Your daydreams and night dreams may seem unimportant, but they can be a valuable source of ideas and creative inspiration for what you want for your couple. In addition to giving you valuable information about your vision for your relationship, you will come to see that sharing your daydreams and night dreams with each other produces a feeling of closeness not readily attainable in our busy lives. Everyone has several dreams each night, even if you don't remember them. By paying attention to them, you will soon be able to start remembering them, and you can then use them to create a vision for your relationship. By sharing and interpreting your dreams together, what we call "co-dreaming," you can increase your closeness and develop plans for your future while having fun in the process.

We did this co-dreaming while on a weekend trip with our family when our children were young. We wanted to make our vacation relaxing and enjoyable, and we also wanted to create a vision of quality time with each other and as a family. On the first night of the trip we agreed to do co-dreaming about the issue. The very next morning we recounted our dreams and then analyzed them, discovering in them solutions and a vision we might not have noticed otherwise. The dream that Peter shared that morning was particularly enlightening: "I wake up and hear some noise in the kitchen at our house. I go down to see what it is. I'm expecting to see our two kids there, but there are four children sitting at the breakfast table—two of each of them. I realize that they're twins, that we have two sets of twins. I'm confused but excited." When we discussed this dream, we realized that our kids appearing as "twin twins" was an indication that they could be twice as responsible as we expected them to be in helping with family tasks. We used this insight to create ways for the kids to help out more with chores, which gave us more time for our couple and for all of us to enjoy being together.

Peter's dream was similar to a dream Phyllis had on a family trip several years later, which seemed to reinforce this new, exciting possibility for the family: "I look out a skylight and see two shooting stars, followed by two smaller shooting stars. I also see a white burst of light similar to fireworks. I'm in awe." When we discussed the dream, we saw that the four shooting stars symbolized our potential as a couple and as members of a family of four. We shared these dreams and possibilities with our children during the trip and held fast to our new expectations when we returned home.

Exercise: Sharing Your Dreams

Before you go to sleep, make a pact to pay attention to your dreams, share them with each other in the morning, and analyze them to gather information that might be useful in developing your couple vision. Put a dream journal and a pen next to both sides of your bed.

When you wake up, each of you write down whatever you remember about your dream, even if it is vague. Write in the present tense, as if you are telling a story, and jot down your feelings about your dream. Share these dreams and feelings with each other and then interpret them in terms of your couple vision. Write down any insights you gain from this exercise as well as any actions you might take.

Sharing daydreams and fantasies

Even though everyone has several dreams a night, you may be one of those people who have trouble remembering them. It takes practice. In the meantime, you can explore your daydreams or fantasies with each other. Think about them separately first, and then write down a scenario in which one of your daydreams or fantasies is realized. Then share your daydreams and fantasies and read your scenarios aloud to each other. Here's a great example.

Diane and Morgan had been married for more than five years and had a two-year-old son. They loved each other, but lately they felt that their relationship lacked the passion and spontaneity they had once enjoyed. They each decided to write down their favorite fantasy for their relationship. Diane wrote: *I see us enjoying a candlelight dinner at a fancy restaurant. We drink champagne, looking deeply into each other's eyes and holding hands under the table. The waiter brings a gooey chocolate dessert with whipped cream, which we share.* Morgan wrote: *I see us sitting by a luxurious pool, drinking mai tais. We take turns rubbing suntan oil on each other. We go in the pool, laughing and splashing each other. We seem so playful and carefree.*

When Diane and Morgan read their fantasies out loud to each other, they were struck by what they had in common: they both wanted to have more fun. They saw themselves having fun together in their fantasies and set about planning how to fulfill these fantasies. Diane was reluctant to leave their son with a sitter, so they planned a weekend away when Morgan's mother could come and stay at their house and look after their child. Within a month, they were drinking champagne and rubbing suntan oil on each other, just like in their fantasies. They envisioned a future in which they were having fun together and then made it happen. Diane and Morgan's creative solution shows how quickly you can break through "what is" and get on with creating "what's possible" for your couple if you come up with a couple vision. All you have to do is use your imagination.

Exercise: Sharing Your Daydreams and Fantasies

Take the time to write down your daydreams and fantasies and share them with each other. Come up with an activity that fulfills one of your daydreams or fantasies, one that you will make happen in the near future, and then broaden your perspective by designing a couple vision for your relationship that will inspire you for life.

Look for a miracle

If nothing else seems to get you to your couple vision, you can always ask for a miracle. But we don't mean a miracle in the usual sense of something out of your control. We have in mind *visioning dreams*. Unlike night dreams or even daydreams, visioning dreams are consciously constructed intentions and images built on the foundation of your actual experiences. Together you can invent a vision for your couple that moves beyond the vague romantic ideal of just living "happily ever after." You can actually imagine in detail and design the present and future as you would like it to be, including goals you would like to accomplish and fantasies you would like to realize. But constructing visioning dreams involves more than just goal setting. It entails developing new ideas for the relationship that both partners commit to as an entity, no matter what obstacles or failures are confronted along the way. That may seem like a miracle in itself! The process can be fun and very creative. Come to it with an open mind and a spirit of wonder.

Exercise: Constructing Your Visioning Dream

If you are having trouble creating a vision for your couple, ask yourself, "If a miracle occurred in our relationship now that enabled it to be exactly as we want it to be, what would our relationship look like?" Let yourself imagine your relationship in detail, without censoring anything. Then share your visioning dream with each other and notice what you feel.

Marianne and Paul had been married for over twenty years. It was the second marriage for both of them. They were in therapy because they were so discouraged about their relationship now that the only outcome they could envision was divorce. Still, they wanted to see if there was any way they could restore the wonderful relationship they once had. During a therapy session, Peter, their therapist, asked them to imagine a miracle, and they both came up with the same one almost immediately: "I want us to love and support each other as we grow old together." Tears came to their eyes as they realized that they both wanted the same thing.

This realization of their joint vision provided the motivation they needed to continue working on their relationship.

Here is an exercise to help you create a joint vision for the future you would like to create with your partner. Start the exercise individually, and then complete it together as you share your lists with each other. You will likely discover that your mutual aspirations will inspire you to action.

Exercise: Creating a Joint Vision

THINK:	If I could have it the way I want it to be, what would our relationship look like now? In one year? In five years? In ten years? In fifteen years?
DO:	On a blank sheet of paper, make five columns and label them The Present, One Year, Five Years, Ten Years and Fifteen Years. In each column write down at least three characteristics of the relationship you envision for that time period.
SHARE:	Compare your charts. Do they have anything in common? How do they differ? Talk about the differences and commonalities. Explore together what your life might be like in the future if you achieve what you are imagining. Acknowledge what you appreciate about your couple at the present moment.

The New Language of Couple

Just imagining a joint vision for your relationship is not enough to sustain your commitment over time. *Wanting* your vision is not enough either. You have to construct your joint vision, and to build a strong structure, you need the right tools. One essential tool is widely available, and it's even free—it is the "power tool" of language. The Dynamic Couple is brought into being and supported by using language in a unique way. First, the Dynamic Couple issues a clear statement of joint goals, a couple vision statement, as a verbal affirmation of the vision the partners have for the couple. In so doing the couple *creates* the relationship, in the same way the entire world was created according to biblical writings: "In the beginning was the Word." *Language* is the cornerstone of the couple vision.

Relationships are akin to organizations, so if we want them to succeed, let's learn from what successful organizations do. Successful organizations know the value of making powerful statements for any project the organization undertakes. They call these "mission statements," and they make sure that all participants in a project are on board with the goals of the mission. Having a clear statement of the goals to be achieved and reaching a mutual agreement about them makes it much more likely that the project will succeed.

One such "organization" is the United States of America. The Founding Fathers described their vision for the nation in the Declaration of Independence as "truths" that were "self-evident." About a hundred years later, Abraham Lincoln brought forth his vision of unity and equality in the Emancipation Proclamation. Both of these documents established a vision by *saying* it was so and *committing* to it. We do not abandon the Emancipation Proclamation whenever we encounter injustice; rather, we rely on the words and fundamental principles therein as motivation to continue pursuing the vision. Similarly, your couple vision statement infuses your relationship with a sense of purpose and commitment in all situations. It articulates the "truths" for your relationship, and this enables you both to remain motivated and committed to the goals you have created.

Producing a couple vision statement may initially be a challenging process, just as composing the Declaration of Independence was for the Founders and penning the Emancipation Proclamation most likely was for Abraham Lincoln. Once you accomplish this, however, you will have something you can always turn to for support in your commitment to lifelong love. The couple vision statement can be life altering. One couple just entering retirement was getting on each other's nerves being at home so much with each other every day. "I can't take this anymore!" the wife exclaimed during a marital therapy session with Peter. He suggested they create a positive couple vision statement for their future, and shortly thereafter they came up with "Our vision is to be active and productive together until we die." Just saying those words together on a regular basis gave them a whole new perspective on what was possible for the rest of their life together.

The bottom line here is that Couple is a way of being, not just a thing to *have* that may come and go. It is not necessary to do any particular thing in order to be committed to Couple; you are clear that you *are* Couple because you have both said you are. Your relationship is not something you found, but an entity you created together with language. It is then a place to come from, not a place to get to. The relationship is not dependent on your individual feelings, circumstances or past experiences, but is based upon the commitment to your joint vision. Being Couple becomes a way of life, not something to achieve, which can be lost or destroyed at any time. What follows are specific guidelines for composing a powerful couple vision statement for your own relationship.

Revisiting your marriage vows

If you have had a marriage or commitment ceremony of some kind, you already have experience stating your couple vision in front of witnesses. You may not remember the exact words, but you said "I do" to something. You might have repeated the traditional words "to have and to hold, for better or for worse, in sickness or in health, till death do us part." Or you might have written your own personal words of commitment and recited them with passion and sincerity on your wedding day. The vows, however, often become vague memories, tucked away with the wedding dress and the album, ignored and forgotten. Even worse, you may not *want* to remember them—like the man we once saw in therapy with his wife who remarked that after they recited their vows and kissed, he said, "Thank goodness, I won't have to do that anymore!" We are still not totally sure what he meant by that, but we are certain it wasn't a good sign for lifelong love.

Forgetting or neglecting the vision you originally had for your marriage can threaten the growth of your relationship. You may not remember the exact wording or still subscribe to your original vows, but it's important to know where you both started in terms of your couple vision. Thus a possible place to begin in creating a fresh couple vision statement is with the vows you exchanged and the other meaningful rituals you engaged in on your wedding day. When speaking about such rituals, we are always reminded of Ann and James, who had two jars of sand at their wedding ceremony, one black and one white. While exchanging their marital vows, they blended together the sand in the jars. When they remembered the ceremony thereafter, the word *unity* and the phrase "blending of our lives together" always came to mind, which powerfully supported their commitment to lifelong love.

Take a look and see if you can find your wedding vows, or try to re-create them. When you revisit your original vows, you may conclude that they sound trite, stale or even obligatory, rather than inspirational. That is a sign that it's time to throw them out and create something new. You can do this by updating and rewriting your vows in a way that more powerfully supports your relationship in the present. Even if you are both satisfied with your original wedding vows, experiment with creating together a new couple vision statement for your relationship. After all, you know each other so much better now and have had so many experiences together. As the late Eric Berne, the renowned psychiatrist, wrote in *Transactional Analysis in Psychotherapy* (1975), "As each spouse emerges in a new form, an opportunity is offered for a psychological remarriage if they both desire it." The opportunity here is to create something brand-new and exciting, something that didn't exist before.

Exercise: Creating a Couple Vision Statement

Together identify any particular words or phrases that contributed to the creation of your relationship. These might be your wedding vows, special quotes about love or even lyrics to a favorite song you both love. Recite those words and phrases aloud together. Take note of those that are still inspiring for you and those that don't seem to fit anymore.

Identify and discard any limiting statements in your vows. Then compose a new statement of your joint couple vision for your relationship, and recite it together. You might even want to reenact your wedding ceremony, reciting your new vows to each other, perhaps in the company of friends or a mentor. Serve food to add a nice touch to the celebration.

Fred and Donna, a couple married for over twenty years, were recovering from a recent infatuation that Fred had with another woman. While in therapy with Phyllis, they rewrote their marital vows, designed a marriage ceremony and practiced it at home. They arranged to reenact their ceremony during a therapy session. Everyone, including Phyllis, dressed up for the occasion and went through the ritual in a formal way. At the end Phyllis sang them their favorite song and they all drank champagne. Everyone had a great time, and Fred and Donna were able to move on from the past and create a new future together.

A nice time to reenact your vows is on your wedding anniversary. On their thirty-fifth anniversary, one couple we came to know went back to the chapel where they were married and renewed their vows. The bride wore the same wedding gown she wore at their original ceremony, and the groom sang "You've Got a Friend" as their friends and family watched. You can also arrange to renew your vows with another couple or a group of couples with anniversaries around the same time. That is what we did one New Year's Day with Robert and Laura. It was their tenth anniversary and our twenty-fifth anniversary. We planned a recitation of each of our vows, rehearsed a quartet version of "Side by Side," along with a little dance, and then had the ceremony at a party given by some couple friends. We all cherish the memories of that day, and other couples who were there still tell us how much the renewing of our vows continues to inspire them.

Exercise: Renewing Your Marriage Vows

Rewrite your original marriage vows, or, if you prefer, you can create entirely new vows. Then plan a renewing your vows ceremony and invite friends and family to share in this occasion with you. Don't forget to take lots of pictures or a video at the ceremony.

What keeps lifelong love alive is not the fact that you created a couple vision statement or renewed your wedding vows, but that you *continue* to revisit your statement and vows. So recite your couple vision statement and marriage vows to each other on a regular basis to reinforce their power in your lives. Doing so in the *present* supports the "life force" of lifelong love. While sharing your couple vision statement and reenacting marital vows are essential, there is another way to keep lifelong love alive that is even more efficient and powerful. It involves creating what we call a *couple proclamation*, the key tool for achieving commitment. The rest of this chapter describes how to design a couple proclamation and use it in your daily life.

Designing a Couple Proclamation

You may have just had a great time re-creating and renewing your vows and formulating and reciting your couple vision statement. Becoming aware of your couple vision is like being "pregnant" with the child you have created together. The next step is to give birth to that child Couple, and to give it a name. The difference between Couple and an actual baby is that Couple is realized completely through language, not biology. Together you have to speak your relationship into being, which, while challenging, is a lot easier than childbirth! And you don't need to worry about your biological clock running out. Proclaiming your couple into being is what sets the Dynamic Couple apart. It is the distinct expression of commitment.

We define a *couple proclamation* as a brief personal statement of commitment to the relationship. The couple proclamation must be agreed to by both partners and typically reinforces the powerful vision for their life together. (A "couple declaration" is a similar tool used in Couples Coaching Couples, described in Chapter Six.) The proclamation is similar to an organization's mission statement for a project, described earlier. You might also think of it as your own personal couple mantra or blessing, a sacred statement repeated over and over. Gurus often give their students their own special mantra. In the same way, you can give each other a shared meaningful statement unique to your couple. To make it a bit easier, rest assured that you will be creating several proclamations during your lifetime as a couple, so there is no pressure to get it "right" the first time.

Robert and Laura were elated that with all their grown children out of the house, they could just relax. They had found the perfect little "honeymoon" cottage beside a babbling brook and declared it "home" for the rest of their lives. Laura wanted to fulfill a long-postponed dream of becoming an art therapist, but it turned out that the graduate program she wanted to enroll in was three thousand miles away. If she were to live her dream, it looked like they would have to leave their beloved home and the community in which they were so invested. Robert did not want to give up his roots and his connection to his large extended family on the East Coast, especially at this stage of his life, and Laura didn't want to sacrifice her lifetime goal for the sake of others, as she had done so many times before. They seemed to be at an impasse. Laura thought she might have to choose between her career and their marriage. They even considered a three-year separation while she went to school.

Then they stopped and looked at what they both really wanted in life. They saw that they were committed most of all to their relationship. Thinking about their couple as an entity, Couple, they realized they did not have to give up home and hearth if they moved; they came to see that in their hearts they were already "home" and inseparable. They composed a proclamation of their commitment: "We are home for each other!" It was their couple that was the foundation of their home, their commitment to each other rather than their attachment to a particular place. They leased their cottage and moved out West together, saying their proclamation every day. They flew back East for family events, returning to stay after five years away. This was all possible only because they saw that their relationship was their home, and that wherever they lived together was an adventure.

Here are the basic principles and procedures for composing your own couple proclamation. Read them all first before starting to work on your proclamation.

Select a suitable setting and clarify your intentions

It is important that both you and your partner give your full attention to the process of creating your proclamation. Just as in giving birth to your child, things will go a lot more smoothly if you are both focused on supporting each other. Find a private location where you are both comfortable and cannot be distracted or interrupted. Unlike the childbirth process, you get to choose the exact time to create your proclamation. Set aside thirty to sixty minutes to devote to this task. Some people like to work on their proclamations at home during a time when they won't be disturbed by children or the telephone; others like to go out for a quiet meal or drive together. One enterprising couple likes to work on their proclamations in the bathtub together, by candlelight. We sometimes like to work on our proclamations after sharing our dreams from the night before, looking at what ideas the dreams suggest for a new proclamation. That is what we did with Phyllis's "Shooting Stars" dream described earlier. From that dream we created the proclamation "We are shooting stars." That proclamation, and the very image of shooting stars, inspired us every day for a few months to create and maintain a powerful way of life for our whole family.

No matter where and when you choose to work on creating your proclamation, be sure that you intend to create a mutually supportive environment in which to work. You can do that by discussing the vision you have for your relationship, and by telling each other what you appreciate about your couple at that moment. It also helps to look at what issues are currently important in your life and any challenges you are facing. You don't want to have a proclamation that is designed to "fix" something, but you certainly can work on creating a way of being that will support your couple in meeting those challenges.

For example, a couple who was dealing with a problematic relationship with their daughter-in-law considered the proclamation "We are nurturing." Then they realized that it was designed to try and fix their relationship with her and that it wasn't very inspiring. They eventually created the proclamation "We are lovers," shifting the focus to nurturing each other to deal with this issue and whatever else they faced in their lives. It inspired them and enabled them to lighten up and have a much more positive attitude about their upcoming visit with their son and daughter-in-law.

Focus on Couple, not individuals

The key element in producing an effective proclamation for your relationship is to make sure that the focus is on Couple, not on each of you as individuals. Using the plural pronoun *we* in your couple proclamation helps to sharpen your focus and perspective. The proclamation does not have to start with or include the word *we,* but that word helps to keep you conscious of your joint task. No matter what issue or project you are taking on, the focus on Couple in the proclamation empowers you and enables you to accomplish whatever it is that you are taking on together.

After Sharon and Ron, who were married and had two young children, took Ron's mother and grandmother into their home to live with them, tension grew between them. Sharon bore the brunt of caring for Ron's relatives, and she started to resent having them there. In therapy with Phyllis, they were clear about their joint vision of being caretakers for their extended family and created the proclamation "We back each other up 100 percent." Once they started saying that proclamation every day, Ron began pitching in more at home, and Sharon felt more positive about the whole situation and their relationship. They worked together to find additional support for caring for the children and his mother and grandmother. Now Sharon was no longer making "I" statements, like "How am I going to handle all this?" Instead they asked together, "How are we going to take care of it?" Learning this new way of speaking is similar to learning a foreign language, like Japanese or Chinese, and we came to call the new language Sharon and Ron were speaking "couplese." At the core of this "couplese" language is the couple proclamation.

Some examples of powerful "we statements" that others have turned into couple proclamations include "We are a winning team," "We trust our couple," "We are a playful dance," "We're up to it" and

"We are soaring together." The statement can simply convey "we" without mentioning that word, as in "Our couple is the source of our love," "The magic is back," "It's all about love" and "It's a privilege being a couple." The possibilities are endless.

Stay positive

Make sure as you start exploring the vision of what you want for your couple that you keep a positive focus. It may be tempting to talk about what's wrong with your relationship right now, to complain and to try to fix problems, but that doesn't work very well. You are likely to go down that hole and get stuck. Rather, think about what you appreciate about each other and your couple and how you want to reinforce that. For instance, you might want to say something like "We enjoy being with each other," as opposed to "We don't complain about each other."

Use the present tense to declare a fact, not a wish

Whatever proclamation you agree on, make sure it is written in the present tense as a declaration of fact, as if it is happening now, not as a wish for the future. It may feel like you are faking it at the moment, but that's okay. Fake it until you make it, as the saying goes. For example, your proclamation might be "We are loving partners" not "We want to be loving partners." After all, you would trust the pilot of your airplane more if s/he said, "We are flying to New York" rather than "We want to fly to New York." Declaring a fact in the present tense inspires more confidence than announcing a hope for the future. You may recognize that such a declaration of fact is similar to what many call an "affirmation," a strong positive statement affirming that something is so. With your proclamation, you are reminding yourself of the commitment you've already made and remembering it right now.

Pay attention to your body language and tone

It's not just what you say that matters; it's how you say it. Repeat your couple proclamation together, looking at each other when you do, and notice what you are both experiencing in the moment. Allow the proclamation to trigger positive feelings as it evokes the vision that inspired it. How will you know if you and your partner are experiencing those feelings? As you say your proclamation and hear it spoken out loud, take note of expressions of excitement or changes in body language in either yourself or your partner. You may notice your partner's face brighten with a smile, the tone of your voice soften, or your bodies lean forward or back. Or you might find that both of you are laughing out loud. You may notice sensations in your body, such as warmth or tingling, which reflect increased excitement, relaxation, satisfaction or joy. Pay attention to these sensations and describe them to each other. Later you may use these experiences as a physical reminder of the power of your proclamation and commitment to Couple.

Adding a gesture to the end of your proclamation can also enhance the impact of your joint expression. For example, you may want to include a hug, a wink, a kiss, a high five, or something of that nature, when you say your proclamation. It can anchor and reinforce your statement and serve as a private signal that you use with each other at opportune times, such as when other people are looking or you don't want to speak out loud.

If you don't notice any positive feelings or sensations when you state your proclamation, keep saying it until the power of the proclamation is present in both the words and your nonverbal expressions. If it still doesn't inspire you both, keep experimenting with different wording and ways of stating your proclamation until you agree that you have something inspiring. Don't accept a so-so statement just to have one. It needs to light you both up, to unite you in your commitment, and it should not be more of the same old dull stuff. Keep at it, and "fake it till you make it." It doesn't matter if it feels true now as long as you are committed to it as a possibility. The only ones to say if it is "true" or not are you two, so you might as well go for it. Other people can be helpful, however, in the process of arriving at a proclamation. A good test of the power of your proclamation is to see if it inspires others. Approach a few people you trust, share your proclamation with them, and notice if it lights them up to hear it. Later you can work with another couple as a coach to create proclamations together. We discuss this more in Chapter Six.

Sometimes just the addition of one word can make all the difference. For example, when working on a writing project together, we tried out the proclamation "We are the source of power and creativity." We noticed that it didn't quite provide the juice we needed to think "big." After working on it some more, we came up with the word *infinite*, which is not a usual word in our vocabulary. When we added it to our proclamation, we could both feel that we had really hit on something that inspired us. The proclamation we finally agreed on—and the one that generated the most excitement and productivity for us—was "We are the source of infinite support, power and creativity." It worked to motivate us, whether we were together, talking on the phone with each other or just saying it to ourselves.

Don't get discouraged if your proclamation isn't "perfect." You are not looking for one that will last forever. You will be creating many of them, and they will build on each other. Just go with something that inspires you both in the moment, and notice how it works for you as you incorporate it into your life. The next section of this chapter tells you how to do this.

Keeping Your Couple Proclamation Alive

The creation of your couple proclamation is not the end of your work on establishing commitment in your relationship, but the beginning. As with a good exercise program, getting clear about your routine is not the end of your physical development; it takes continuous work to build up muscles and keep them in shape. Any skill that is worth having takes attention and effort to maintain. An opera singer, for example, doesn't sing solely at performances; it takes countless hours of practice to prepare for a performance and keep an operatic voice in shape. Here are some simple ways to keep your couple proclamation and love alive. Though these steps are easy to follow and are often a lot of fun, it may not always be easy to do what it takes to stay committed to your vision. It demands consistent work, but the results are certainly worth the effort.

Commit to repetition and practice

What will keep your relationship alive and thriving is not the act of reciting a couple proclamation, but reciting it continually. Once is definitely not enough when it comes to stating your proclamation. You will forget about it quickly, and it can disappear in a nanosecond when you are in "the heat of battle." So make reciting your proclamation a ritual, like brushing your teeth, and be sure to do it at least once a day and preferably twice, usually at the beginning and end of each day. Your proclamation is a powerful reminder of what you are committed to in your life together. It may feel awkward or silly to say it over and over, but it will become second nature after a while. Like learning any new language, it generally takes some time to feel comfortable with it.

It is best to say your proclamation when you are physically together, but that may not always be possible. If you are not in the same place, you can repeat it together on the telephone or even leave it as a message on each other's phones or via your favorite method of communication (email, texting and so on). We often add it to any message we leave each other, just as a reminder of what we are about. On one occasion when Peter took some time out to conduct business during our vacation at the beach, we touched base by cell phone and both stood in the ocean, but on different stretches of the beach, and recited our proclamation together. It was very romantic and reaffirmed our togetherness even though we were apart.

Experiment with reciting your proclamation in different ways. Sometimes you may want to hold hands when you say it. You may also try emphasizing a different word in your proclamation, starting with the first one and then doing each word in turn. Take note of the nuances this adds to your proclamation. It may reveal some things you hadn't noticed before. Even if it feels awkward or silly to say the proclamation, keep at it. Let it grow on you each day. You will get used to it very soon and will even find that you miss it if you don't say it one day. Don't wait for the other person to initiate it or blame your partner if you forget to say your proclamation. Each of you is equally responsible for reciting it. Work out a way that supports your couple to remember, like creating a routine or cue to remind you.

Create a concrete representation of the proclamation

Often spoken words are not enough to keep a proclamation alive. All of us rely on a variety of senses in our experience (touching, seeing, hearing, tasting and smelling) to help us remember things.

As we noted before, gestures added to the proclamation help reinforce it, especially for people who are more visual. In addition, a concrete, physical representation of the proclamation, a tangible reminder that one can look at and touch, helps to make the proclamation more real. Tangible reminders are effective in combating the phenomenon of "out of sight, out of mind," a real pitfall for couples no matter how powerful a proclamation may be. It is important to come up with something that you both can relate to and incorporate into your daily life.

One of the easiest ways to create a physical representation of your proclamation is to write it on sticky notes, which can be placed strategically around your house, office and car. One couple we know put their proclamation on the screen saver of their laptops. They found that it not only helped them focus on their relationship, but also fostered a more positive attitude toward their work. When we give greeting cards to each other on birthdays and holidays, we add our proclamation below our signatures. Peter even has the word *Couple* on his license plate, which reminds us and tells the world about our ultimate proclamation. There are lots of ways to display your proclamation. Choose those that suit your couple best.

A fun thing to do is to make a collage together that represents your proclamation. Collect pictures from magazines, favorite photos, quotations and paper mementos, and affix them to poster board to make a collage about your relationship. Put the item that has a very special meaning for both of you, like a favorite picture or quote, at the center of the collage and build around that. Then display the collage somewhere where you both will see it frequently. If you have young children, you may want to invite them to join you in the collage-making process. It's good modeling, and it provides support for your couple. You may even find that your kids remind you to say your proclamation or even want to say it with you. It may feel awkward for you at first, but young children love being part of this and even older kids seem to appreciate it. The teenage son of one couple we know even went out and created a proclamation with his girlfriend after hearing what his parents were doing.

In addition to making things yourselves, you may also want to buy things related to your proclamation. We have taken to purchasing what we call "couple art," paintings and sculptures that represent Couple to us in a positive way. We display these items around the house, and it serves to remind us of our various proclamations over time, as well as our commitment to Couple in general. One of our favorites is a sculpture of two dolphins swimming next to each other. It sits on a shelf across from our bed, and we get to begin and end every day with that symbol of our lifelong love. Sounds romantic—and it is, even after all this time.

Don't forget about the other senses. The most powerful sense for inducing memory is smell. You may want to go out shopping together for a fragrant perfume, lotion or massage oil that speaks to your current proclamation. Music also enhances memory. Try to think of a song or some meaningful music that relates to your proclamation in an inspiring way. Then get it and play or sing it together or to each other. It can become "your song." Whenever Phyllis, an opera singer by vocation, gives a performance, she always dedicates a love song to Peter and their couple. She loves the way it lights him up to hear it. You don't have to be an opera singer to sing romantic songs to your partner. Just have fun with it, maybe even in the shower.

Exchange gifts to reinforce your proclamation

One couple we met dined at an Indian restaurant from time to time because the husband especially liked Indian food. The wife was not such a fan of this cuisine, but she happily went to reinforce their proclamation "We support each other." The husband felt greatly supported by her effort. He said it was like she was giving him a gift each time they went to the Indian restaurant together. You might think of gifts that represent your proclamation that you can give to each other, such as poems, flowers, an afternoon outing or an evening of theater. There's really no end to the gifts you can exchange to reinforce your proclamation. Be generous to your couple, and the presents will keep appearing.

Create a new proclamation every few months

The final step in keeping your proclamation alive is to create new proclamations. While you may love your first ever proclamation, don't get too attached to it. It is likely to outlive its usefulness and lose its vitality after a few months. This is actually good. It gives you the opportunity to experience the fun and excitement of re-creating your vision together again. Old proclamations never have to die or go away completely, however. Find a convenient spot where you list all your proclamations. We put each new proclamation on label tape, and then we post the label-tape proclamation on our refrigerator with the others. In this way, we get to look at all our proclamations every day if we want to. They are a nice reminder of the road we have traveled, and gazing at them is a lot less fattening than opening the refrigerator!

Once you have created your first couple proclamation, the next ones will likely come more easily. You will already know the process, and it is just a matter of looking at what's going on in your life and the challenges you are facing at the moment. Designing a new proclamation for your couple doesn't mean there is anything wrong with your relationship the way it is; rather, it is a way to make your commitment even stronger, and to provide support for each other as you tackle the current issues and challenges in your life together. You will come to see that the more attention you give to your proclamations, the more you will strengthen and reinforce the commitment you have made to each other and the more you will enrich your relationship, which is a dynamic and growing entity. Proclamations, in other words, contribute to your versatility, flexibility and vitality as a couple. This vitality is what keeps lifelong love alive in the face of our natural desire for security and predictability. In long-term relationships, we all need to experience a sense of certainty. However, that same need can kill the excitement and passion of a relationship. Fortunately, continually creating new proclamations for your couple will reenergize your relationship and deepen the passion and the commitment you feel for each other.

A great example of how successive proclamations work to keep a relationship alive is Robert and Laura's experience. We mentioned earlier their proclamation "We are home for each other" and how it enabled them both to feel comfortable about the decision to leave their house and move across country for Laura's graduate work. But that was just their first challenge and their first proclamation related to this new adventure. They soon realized that the only way to manage this transition was to have a long-distance relationship for a few months. Then they would live together again. For that period of separation, they created the proclamation "We are creative, fearless adventurers." It helped them figure out ways to support each other in their respective locations. Once they were together again and they were tackling their own careers, they designed the proclamation "We are an expansive couple and are proud of each other." This helped motivate them both to meet the challenges of being in a new place together with new responsibilities.

Looking back at a series of proclamations we made in the course of one year not too long ago, we were able to see how our confidence grew as we took on new challenges. We started the year with the proclamation "We are way up there," then moved on to "We are soaring," "We are up to it" and, finally, "We are over the top." We started where we were at the moment—which is all any of us can do at any given time—and then progressed from there. Upping the ante with each successive proclamation that year helped us to feel more confident and to meet our goals along the way—until the next challenge and the next proclamation came along.

Proclamation-making is an ongoing process that supports living happily ever after in lifelong love. It is crucial that you work on establishing a sense of commitment in your relationship and have a couple proclamation before you move on to the second C of Couple Power, cooperation, which is discussed in Chapter Four. Keep refining your couple proclamation until you find something you can both agree on, and then build from there. If you are still stuck, you may want to consult a marriage counselor or a therapist to help you sort it out. (We deal more with the issue of when to consult a therapist in Chapter Eight.) Here is an exercise to help you through the process of creating your own couple proclamation. Have fun with it.

Exercise: Designing a Couple Proclamation

Set aside about thirty minutes to do this exercise. Find a quiet place where you won't be interrupted.

THINK:	Think about the vision you have for your couple and your commitment to it. Think about the challenges you face in your life now.
DO:	Discuss your couple vision, your commitment and the challenges you must tackle with your partner. Write down inspiring words and phrases related to these topics that you both agree upon. Now condense your words and phrases into one short and simple sentence. Follow these guidelines:

- Make your proclamation couple-focused.
- Keep it positive.
- State it as fact in the present tense, not as hope for the future.
- Make sure it inspires both of you.
- Say your proclamation together (looking at each other).
- Make any changes you deem necessary.
- Write down the proclamation on sticky notes and display these in prominent places.

SHARE:	Say your couple proclamation together at least twice a day.

CHAPTER FOUR

Cooperation:

The Second Step toward Lifelong Love

"When spouses work cooperatively toward some end, or to fulfill some purpose, their cooperation draws them together and enhances their emotional experience."

—Blaine Fowers, *Beyond the Myth of Marital Happiness*

Couple—The Ultimate Team

Being committed to your relationship is the foundation of lifelong love. Commitment entails a vow or a promise you and your partner make to be together as a unit, but lifelong love requires more than just a promise. You need to *act* as Couple in accordance with the vision you created together. What does acting as Couple look like? First and foremost, it looks like two people who have mastered the art of cooperation. In essence, cooperation is "love in action."

Being in a relationship is like being part of a team, and it's the team that acts most effectively as a unit that is most likely to win. The more effort team members devote to teamwork, the more power they can harness to reach their goal. As many coaches will tell you, it is not just having the best players on your team that wins championships; it is being the best at working together. Think about mules climbing a steep hill together; they instinctively lean into each other to help manage the burden. And geese flying in formation for great distances take turns flying at the head of the "V" and resting at the back. In other words, each member of the team cooperates to ensure the best outcome.

Most of us think we are good at cooperating, but few of us actually are. Operating as a team is not natural for the majority of us, and it requires a great deal of coaching and practice. True cooperation as a couple can be difficult, but it is very rewarding. Here is an example. Dan and Myra, the couple we met in Chapter One, had been through a lot together. Theirs was the second marriage for each of them, and they helped each other heal after difficult first relationships. They described themselves as "happy but not necessarily joyful." One of the issues they struggled with was Myra's weight. They agreed that it would be healthy for her to lose weight and that this would be good for their relationship. She would feel better about herself, and Dan would feel more attracted to her. Myra knew that Dan was supportive, but she felt that he was more critical than helpful. He seemed to think that it was up to her to lose the weight. Nothing happened for years. She became resentful and resigned to being overweight, and Dan was convinced that he was destined to have a pudgy wife. Dan and Myra were not really cooperating as a couple. They were waiting for the other person to do something decisive.

Dan spoke to one of his friends about his frustration regarding Myra's weight. His friend suggested that Dan and Myra talk about it together and see what they could come up with as a team. They arranged to speak about Myra's weight problem one Saturday afternoon. It was a beautiful sunny day, so they had their talk while taking a walk. As they laughed and acted playful, they remembered walking on the beach together during their last vacation. Dan suggested that while they were in such a good mood, they could brainstorm some ideas about what would keep their relationship "light and fun." The topic of Myra's weight came up when she said she was not feeling very "light."

Dan had this idea first, but Myra loved it right away: they would take on her weight problem together as a team. They went to a local weight loss clinic and joined together. Each week they were to weigh in and assess their progress. Both of them had some weight to lose, but rather than finding out how each of them had done individually every week, they decided to ask the clinic to reveal only their combined weight loss as a couple. In that way, they would see how their "team" was doing. Guess what? They lost a great deal of weight, thanks especially to Myra, and regained their joy and romance. After the weight issue was handled, they were able to focus on the deeper issues of intimacy that they had been ignoring. They could approach these more difficult concerns as a team, knowing better now how to cooperate and work together on them. Dan and Myra had been acting like a Romanticized Couple without the romance. They were obsessed about romance not being there. Their physical attraction had diminished, but they did care about each other. As they began to cooperate about the weight and other issues, they experienced a new attraction to each other. They became excited about their progress, looked at each other differently and had a good feeling about their common goal.

Most people don't know how to get past their own self-interest to cooperate with their partner, and they don't see the price they are paying for that. They don't know how to find a way to be together that satisfies them both, that does not involve self-sacrifice or compromise, a feeling of giving up something. When couples first get together, they generally think they are acting cooperatively, but actually they may not have the experience or the skills to know how to cooperate effectively. Just "doing stuff" together isn't necessarily cooperation. Real cooperation requires completing a number of important tasks, and having the skills to do so. Establishing common objectives and goals and a vision for the couple is a start. This is accomplished by creating a powerful couple proclamation and then developing joint project plans and contracts (described later in this chapter). Once these tasks are performed, you will see that you can keep inventing new ways of working together. You will experience the power and satisfaction of shared accomplishments.

Cooperation Versus Compromise

The first step in developing the skill of cooperation is to understand the difference between cooperation and compromise. Cooperation involves the creation of something new *together,* not just agreeing to do what the other person wants. The dictionary defines *cooperation* as a "joint operation or action" or the "willingness to assist." But when embarking on a joint action, you may believe that you will be forced to compromise, that is, to give in to the other's wishes or to give up what you really want, or you may be afraid that you will become overly dependent upon your partner. If that happens, you might feel vulnerable to being let down, used, abandoned or disappointed. Cooperation requires trust at a very basic level. You must be willing to take a risk.

Frank and Andrea, a Self-Focused Couple, had been married for more than fifteen years and had a very loving relationship. They were raising three young children together effectively. Both of them held down responsible jobs in large companies. However, Andrea often felt that Frank did not trust her to do certain things or take the lead in joint projects at home. For example, shortly after they bought a ski boat, Andrea noticed that Frank drove the boat almost all the time. When it came time for him to water-ski, he would do so only if a male friend was at the helm. On one occasion, one of his male friends asked Frank, "Doesn't Andrea ever drive the boat?" On the way home that day Andrea asked Frank why he drove the boat all the time. He said that she did not know how to drive it very well. At that point they made a commitment to share more equally in the water-skiing by having Andrea learn how to drive the boat. Andrea, who had less boating experience, said she wanted to learn everything there was to learn about taking care of the boat and driving it. Frank spent time instructing her, and they cooperated fully.

The next time they went out in the boat, Frank was on water skis, completely at the mercy of Andrea's driving. He had a choice right then to trust her or not. He chose to trust his partner and just lean back and relax. Andrea pushed the throttle forward, and he sprang out of the water. She did very well, and she could see him smiling at her when she turned to look back. When he returned to the boat, they were both jumping up and down. They were so happy. Their cooperation generated a feeling of togetherness and victory. They had created something new together; they felt like a couple who together could do anything. Now cooperation was possible in so many other things. Andrea felt like a full partner in their relationship, and Frank saw how important it was to Andrea to feel acknowledged as an equal and how it supported their couple to trust each other. On the way home, they talked about buying a double kayak and having Andrea play a larger role in planning their retirement. Frank felt a burden lift off of him, and Andrea felt like a full contributor to their future.

Building a Team

To win a team championship, there must be more than hope or luck. If a sports team wants to win, it must cultivate dedication and discipline, and it must do things consistently over time. The team called Couple requires the same thing. To begin to work as a team, you must first decide the purpose of your team. What goal would you like to achieve? At the first team practice, a coach may write on the chalkboard "National Championship" or "The World Cup." Now the team members know what they are aiming for. What are you aiming for? To emerge as a "championship" couple, you must have a vision for your team and set goals together.

Setting goals

Remember Mildred and Richard, the Traditional Couple discussed earlier? They were married for thirty-nine years. Richard had a successful career in management, and now at age sixty-six, he wanted to retire. Mildred, as you recall, had been waiting for "her turn" to have the career she wanted. Mildred's turn had never materialized, and she was unhappy. Richard's plan to retire and be underfoot was not what she had hoped for. There had been some cooperation along the way, but it was not as conscious partners. She had been compromising, not really cooperating, agreeing to do whatever he wanted while secretly resenting it. Neither of them had given all that they could to the relationship. The dilemma for them was how to create a new vision for their relationship that was exciting and enlivening for both of them. Now in couples therapy was their chance to do that.

They began by reaffirming their commitment to the relationship. Once they did that, they were able to create an empowering couple proclamation: "We are powerful together." The task for them was to put their commitment into action through cooperation. They began to schedule time together to plan a project that would express their commitment to their marriage. It was almost like one of Richard's executive committee meetings. They took over the dining room table, brought out a bunch of legal pads, took notes and drank coffee. He loved to run things and think about marketing and sales strategies. She wanted to use some of her skills in interior design and architecture. They both loved people. Mildred, most especially, wanted to be among adults, talk about interesting issues and hear about their lives. They both also agreed that they wanted a new house. They took all of this into consideration as they cast about for a project.

One day in the real estate section of the newspaper, they saw a house on the water that was not far from where they lived. *Too big,* they thought. It could fit three or four families. Then, almost at the same moment, the idea for a bed-and-breakfast came to both of them. The B and B gave them a common goal to achieve. They got right to work. Richard started looking for financing, while Mildred thought about where she could get furnishings to fit the historical period of the house. He looked into the permits they would need, and she started visiting other bed-and-breakfasts. They both had a new sense of purpose, and every evening they would meet to share their progress. They worked together for the next two years to build a successful B and B, which attracted people from all over the region, and, in the process, their marriage became stronger than it had ever been.

Coaching

Think about great sports teams. They often have great players, but they always have outstanding coaches. Sometimes we hear about teams with great players that can't seem to win. The coaches get blamed for not making the athletes play like a team. And sometimes you hear about teams with no real "stars" winning championships. Coaches often get the credit for that. Coaching makes a difference. Coaches frame the vision of the team and devise the best strategies to reach the team's goal. They seek to maximize the contributions of the players, to push them beyond where they have gone before. Coaches can make a vital contribution to your couple by teaching you how to cooperate more effectively. We explain more about what coaches and coaching do for couples in Chapter Six.

Victor and Harriet met in graduate school, in a doctoral seminar. They fell in love and got engaged. Each was writing a thesis at the time, and a lot of their hours were taken up doing research and working alone on their mammoth projects. After about six months, they realized that neither of them was making much progress in their writing. It was clear they needed to do something to move forward. They asked a friend who had recently completed his dissertation for advice. Their decision to get some outside help was the product of a conversation they had about the fear they each had that if they did not finish their degrees, they would never feel like an equal in their relationship, and it would be like they had to give something up in order for the other to succeed. Their friend spent time coaching them separately but soon decided that it would work better to coach them together as a couple. Not only was it more efficient for him, but he also saw that there was some power that Harriet and Victor had as a couple that would allow them to support each other more fully. They shared with each other the work they had completed on their theses and made suggestions. Within six months, both of their theses were complete, and they had obtained teaching jobs in the same city. Coaching helped Harriet and Victor develop as a team.

Practicing

Anyone who has ever been on a team is familiar with practice. Practice helps with coordination, communication and competency. We also use practice time to build strength, capacity and familiarity. There are at least two kinds of practice. The first involves a team's preparation for something in the future, such as a project, a performance or a game. It entails going through motions or routines over and over again, learning them and teaching our bodies and our minds to do things we are not used to doing. This kind of practice trains our bodies and minds to operate in a particular way, and it involves working with another person to learn about their reactions and tendencies so we can operate "as one" with them. For the team called Couple, it means being clear about your goal and working toward it consistently. Think of rowing a boat together. Each person has individual strength, but if the strokes are not synchronized, some power is wasted. Pulling together harnesses the power of both people, but this takes practice. When we get into a relationship, it is akin to going from rowing two separate boats to rowing one larger boat together. The potential exists to go faster together than either partner could alone, but this requires coordination and cooperation. And coordination and cooperation hinge on practice and rehearsals.

Joe and Jane were in their thirties when they got married. She had been married for a few years right out of college but then got divorced. About ten years later, she met Joe for the first time at a chamber of commerce event in their city. By now she was an established realtor and he was an established builder. They fell in love and were married within six months. At first, they were worried that their careers would not leave them much time to spend together. Joe had to be at job sites early, and Jane often worked evenings and weekends. She was resentful that he was too tired to participate in evening activities, and he thought she was never around when he had free time. With busy careers, Joe and Jane struggled to find time together. But ironically, it was through work that they discovered how cooperation could strengthen their relationship.

At another chamber of commerce meeting, they took on a project together that required a builder and a realtor. Along with a few other people, they worked on a project to develop some houses in a new neighborhood. One of the things they needed to do for their joint project to be successful was to attract investors. Even though Joe was a bit shy, they agreed they would meet with investors together. They set up a meeting at Jane's office for just the two of them, then sat down together and wrote out what each of them would say and then practiced it. Within a week, they had a number of investors lined up. Jane and Joe were delighted with what they had accomplished and had a renewed sense of themselves as Couple. They decided to have a meeting every week and to look at their schedules and find more time to be together. After a while, their regularly scheduled meetings became fun for them. They would experiment with meeting in different coffee shops, but always at the same time. At the meetings, they would practice dividing up the labor on joint projects and would decide to do some of the work together.

The second kind of practice is a regular activity performed to get to a particular state of readiness or enlightenment. The regular practice of meditation, visualization, yoga and the like creates the opportunity to achieve an internal state of centeredness and satisfaction. This second kind of practice is more about being prepared for all of life and is applicable to the realm of relationships. For Jane and Joe, their weekly meeting became a kind of meditation. While they accomplished things and planned for the future, they also experienced simply being together in a state of equilibrium.

Dori and Judd, a Romanticized Couple, met in high school. They had a brief relationship and then went their separate ways for a few years. They saw each other at their fifth high school reunion and fell in love all over again. They moved in together and were married a year later. He worked long hours at a local bank, and she was a computer programmer for a very large company. Their jobs placed a lot of time pressure on them. They often would not get home from work until after nine at night and would collapse in bed. On the weekends, there were chores to do. She kept the house, and he worked in the yard and fixed up their old duplex. All they seemed to be doing was either working or sleeping. While they enjoyed each other's company immensely, it seemed like they just did not have enough time to be together. Even when they did find a little bit of time, they had to discuss the bills or something that had to be done with relatives or around the house.

At the suggestion of some friends, they began to force themselves to take a few minutes almost every night and have "tea for two." No matter how late it was, they had a cup of tea together, with the express intent of listening to each other. They didn't problem solve or talk about chores; they just spent time being with each other. Some nights they would just hold hands across the table without saying anything for a while, performing a kind of meditation. Other nights they would start out by taking ten deep breaths together. They got to like this meditative exercise, and it became part of their daily routine. Even when Judd would travel for business, they would talk on the phone every night, starting with their ten deep breaths together. They noticed that they were both more relaxed and centered—and they even were able to find more time to be together—because of their practice of "tea for two."

Exercise: Having Tea for Two

Set aside twenty minutes one night a week to have "tea for two," or its equivalent, perhaps coffee for two or wine for two. Do not use the time to discuss the mundane tasks of everyday life, such as household chores or bill paying. Just talk about your relationship and what it means to you, or use the time to meditate together.

Defining roles and expectations

In a team, it is important not only to set goals but also to assign roles to each person and spell out what is expected. On some sports teams, participants play specific positions, such as goalie, quarterback or designated hitter. Each position requires particular skills, and some members of the team may have better skills in certain areas than in others. On a basketball team, for instance, each of the five players is not expected to score one fifth of the points. Some players score points, others are better at getting rebounds and others may have greatest proficiency at passing or playmaking. The same is true in an intimate relationship. The team may be best served by one of you cooking and the other cleaning the gutters on the house. In fact, having each of you specialize in particular "areas" might make for better overall results—what might be viewed as incompatibility may, in fact, provide a greater likelihood of accomplishing the goals you've set.

Carmen and Theresa were fixed up on a blind date after college by a mutual friend. When she arranged the match, she told them both that she didn't think they were actually very compatible. She must have been on to something else, however, because Carmen and Theresa got together, dated for five years or so, and then, after living together for two more years, got married. Carmen was a geek with a great feel for computers, video games and crossword puzzles. His ideal weekend activity was reading the *New York Times* in bed and leafing through the pages of a computer magazine. Theresa was, by contrast, athletic and outdoorsy. She loved to get up early and go for a run for an hour or so, make a smoothie and try to get Carmen out of bed. They seemed so different. He was a couch potato, and she was moving all the time. The issue of their differences came up when they started to plan a vacation together. She wanted to go to a remote mountain resort, and he wanted a place with advanced internet access. She wanted to go hiking, and he wanted to have the *New York Times* delivered to the room. He was not that interested in what she was doing and vice versa. Then an interesting thing happened.

One day, while walking through the mall together on their way to a movie—after finally finding one they both wanted to see—they passed by a camera store. In the window, they saw a high-tech camera and some photo software. They went in and looked. To their surprise, they were both intrigued. Neither of them had any experience with photography, but they felt compelled to explore. They went for coffee and pondered the prospect of developing a hobby together. After coffee they went back to the store and bought a camera for Carmen. A week later they bought another one for Theresa and started planning a trip around their new hobby. Theresa was great at finding places with breathtaking scenery, and Carmen learned how to use new software to make online photo albums.

Their trip was the best they'd ever taken together. Theresa would hike in the mornings to spots where the views were the best, and Carmen would get the cameras ready and update the camera software. Theresa would pack a lunch and off they went.

At night they would look at their pictures over beer and pick the ones they liked. They each contributed their unique talents to their hobby, and they began to have fun together and appreciate each other. Their skills and habits were no longer incompatible; they were complementary, and they began to enjoy their marriage in a way they'd never thought possible.

Training regimens

Not only do sports teams have to practice, but they also need training schedules—time in the gym to work on conditioning and to have planning sessions, or "chalk talks." Couple teams are the same. Training regimens require discipline, dedication and regularity. Create your own training regimen by having a regular date night every week, a lunch together during the week or even a "nooner" once a month or so. These regular occasions to renew intimacy or just be together in a different setting strengthen a relationship. Sometimes they require cooperation, the coordination of plans or advance planning. You might want to alternate the responsibility for arranging the schedule, such as by having each of you plan a surprise activity once a month. Working together to plan activities with other couples—card games, dinners, theater parties—will also enrich your couple life. (Creating a sense of community with other couples is discussed in Chapter Six.)

Ranata and Del had a number of big fights regarding working around the house. Del had a small home-repair business but never seemed to fix anything around their own house. Ranata complained that he thought other people's houses were more important then their own. He wondered why she didn't do some of that stuff herself. She asked, "Why should I, when you are so good at it?" One weekend they went on a trip with their church to help rebuild a religious school building at a rural church about six hours away. They worked together all day Saturday and Sunday repairing flood damage in one of the classrooms. Ranata was impressed with how thoughtfully and carefully Del did her work, and he noticed that she worked incredibly hard and made very helpful suggestions to him. They enjoyed themselves so much that when the weekend was over, they signed up to do another trip three months later. On the way back home on the church bus, they decided that one Saturday a month they would take on one room in their own house and work on improving it the way they had the school classroom. When they got home, they took out a calendar for the entire year and penciled in all their appointments to do repairs together on the different rooms in their house.

Team spirit

Members of successful teams often describe an intangible element at work, what they call team chemistry or team spirit. Some couples, too, describe a certain kind of feeling they get not just from love but from cooperation. Sometimes they feel it following a crisis or challenge of some kind—maybe after surviving a flood in the basement or dealing with a family illness or just getting the taxes in on time. They are proud to have worked together to survive or do something extraordinary. Remember Victor and Harriet who worked hard to get their advanced degrees and secure jobs together? They experienced added satisfaction and joy knowing they had accomplished their goals together. When they marched at graduation, they were as proud of their couple's accomplishment as they were of their own individual achievements. There were "high fives" all around.

Cooperating when apart

It is one thing to get together and cooperate for a big event, a game, a wedding or a business deal, but it is quite another to cooperate on an ongoing basis, even in times of separation. Often couples spend time apart, traveling for business, devoting extra hours to sick relatives or managing a move to a different city, such as when one partner goes ahead to start a job and the other follows with the family later. Sometimes separation may just be taking a trip with your girlfriends or going on a fishing trip with your buddies.

What we have learned over the past three decades is that while a break of some kind or a change in routine can be helpful for a short period of time, the teams that do best are the ones that continue to work on themselves even when the members are separated. Couple can always be present. Remember that being Couple is not a drain on you, but a source of empowerment. There is no real "off season," just a different way to be together. It is not a good or bad thing to be physically separated; it is how we choose to handle the time apart. We can cooperate without being together. While it is not necessary to have daily contact, it may be useful to be on the same page.

Irv and Cookie have been married for forty-two years. He is a practicing dentist nearing retirement, and she is an artist. They have grown children and a few grandchildren as well. For the past ten years or so, Cookie has taken three months every winter to go to France to study with her art teacher. Irv has stayed home to make money in the practice. Cookie is serious about her time in Paris, painting and studying every day with her mentor and going to art museums. Irv and Cookie agreed to this agreement years ago. They work on keeping their relationship alive while they are in different places. Cookie used to write long letters to Irv while in Paris. Now she texts him every day, reporting on her activities, her feelings and her experiences. He responds as often as he can, usually four times a week, and this past year they began to use a computer video system to talk regularly. During Cookie's absence, they are not taking time off from their relationship; they are merely having different experiences and sharing them through correspondence. Irv, for his part, uses Cookie's time away to catch up on his favorite hobby, fishing. Every weekend he goes fly-fishing with his friends. He now emails Cookie pictures of the fish he catches. (Otherwise she would never believe his fish stories!) When they are reunited after three months of separation, they feel like they know what has been going on in each other's lives. They don't need to catch up; they just resume the life they have when they are physically together.

Getting Results

We cooperate with others to enhance our working relationships and also to get results. When we actually have something to show for our efforts, we experience pride and a sense of accomplishment. When couples cooperate effectively, the fruits of their labor give them confidence that they are doers and problem solvers. When something has been produced and a goal has been reached, they are encouraged to take on new tasks and also have some reassurance that they can succeed as a team. When problems arise, they can say, "We have dealt effectively with bigger things than this."

Honest appraisals

One of the difficulties many couples have when assessing their accomplishments is being clear about what has been done. Objectively seeing what has been accomplished is harder than it seems.

There is often so much drama in couple interactions regarding the importance of meeting goals that the partners are not sure what success looks like in concrete terms. If the goal for the relationship is "being happy" or having better communication, it may not be obvious how one determines if the goal has been met.

When it is time to decide what you want to achieve or do together as a couple, it is very important that you and your partner reach a consensus about what success is. You need to clarify before you begin how things will appear when you are finished so you can declare "mission accomplished." For instance, if you decide together to fix up the basement, remodel the bathroom or clean out the garage, what will those areas have to look like for you to say you have succeeded? Maybe there are milestones to achieve along the way or steps to complete. It sounds a bit burdensome to approach the joy of cooperating by focusing on just what has to be done, but it is essential that you both be clear about your expectations. Setting up a project to work on, or just planning a night out together, needs to include some discussion of what the finished product will look like so that both parties' expectations are met.

Keeping agreements

In order for cooperation to work, you must say what you are going to do and then actually do it. It is easy to get carried away and commit to doing things you merely hope you can do without thinking about whether or not you can actually do them. You might agree to do things you know you can't do, perhaps because you want to be nice or you don't think you will be expected to deliver. To truly cooperate with your partner, you must agree to follow through on what you say you will do. That does not mean that you can never break a promise; it only means that if you know that you will not be able to keep your word, you let your partner know. It is like packing a parachute to use when jumping out of a plane together. If you aren't sure you did your part correctly, the time to share that information with your partner is as soon as you know it, not after you jump. It must be understood when cooperating that everyone is doing their best, and that means being honest and asking for support if you need it. Make a promise to work on something, and then be honest about how it is going while it is happening, not later. It takes real trust and courage to do this sometimes. We all want to look good and never break a promise, but when cooperating, you must act like your lives depend upon it. Sharing what you are actually doing in relation to what you promised to do is essential. The skills needed to communicate clearly in your sharing are covered in the next chapter.

Jude and Les were having a party at their apartment. It was the first time they were going to meet the people in their building. They had been in a relationship for about a year but had just moved in together. They divided up the tasks that needed to be completed when setting up the party. Jude agreed to come home early from work to clean up the place, and Les took on the last-minute shopping, promising to bring home what was needed for the bar and the appetizers. They had not planned anything too elaborate, but they wanted it to be well presented.

Les forgot that there was a retirement party for one of his coworkers that day, and it would likely include going out for drinks after work. He planned to stop at the store after sharing a drink with his coworkers to pick up what was on the shopping list. One thing led to another, and Les stayed an hour later than he had intended at the bar, realized he was late and rushed home, forgetting about his assigned task. He got home about twenty minutes before the guests were to arrive, with no bar supplies and no appetizers. Les had time to run out and get some of the things he'd promised to pick up. Jude was very angry. It was not so much that Les broke his promise as much as it was that he did not let her know ahead of time. If Jude had known, she could have made other arrangements so they'd be ready for the party. The arrangement they made in their partnership, as many couples do, was to keep each other informed so they could deliver on their agreements. Telling your partner what is really going on shows that you respect the relationship. Even if you feel foolish or ashamed that you did not keep your promise, it is important to share the news and then deal later with the broken promise.

Ask for what you need

When you and your partner are operating as a team, it is important to trust each other and know when to ask for what you need. In the culture of individualism in which we live, trusting someone else may seem a bit risky. You may fear being used or taken advantage of, and you may be very careful about what you say, do and ask for. This limits your ability to cooperate, because you don't have all the information you need to succeed. Take time to get clear about what you really want for yourself and your couple. If you think about how a team works best, it is when the players ask for what they need, keeping the success of the whole enterprise in mind. A soccer player breaks free, running toward the goal; a wide receiver notices his defender slip. What do they do? They call for the ball. They make a request based on their view of what is needed for the team. Don't be afraid to make a request of your partner. It builds trust and is for the good of the team and your relationship. Without asking, there is little receiving.

Paula and Phil had been feeling distant from one another lately. They went to see Peter for therapy and at his suggestion they went to a weekend couples retreat at a local Outdoor Challenge Center.

One of the exercises they were given on retreat was to stand on two long wires stretched parallel on the ground and to move from one end to the other together. It required them to lean into each other with just the right amount of pressure so as to stay balanced. At first, it seemed like an impossible task. Phil is very tall, and Paula is short. Placing their hands above their heads, they faced each other and leaned in, making a tepee shape with their bodies. Paula had to push hard but was knocked off the wire by his weight. They tried again and again without much success. Phil noticed that they had not spoken a word to each other the whole time; they were just trying and failing. When they started asking each other to change positions one way or another, they were finally able to achieve balance on the wires. Paula said, "Phil, my hands are too high. I can't push against yours." He lowered his hands. He said, "Lean in more. I got you." And Paula did. In this way they were able to keep their balance.

After that weekend they noticed they began to make these same kinds of requests in their daily interactions. They began to strike a "balance" in their life at home and to feel closer to each other as they continued making these requests. For instance, Paula told Phil that she wanted him to take out the garbage on Mondays without having to remind him every time. He told her he hadn't known that it bothered her so much and that she could count on him to do that regularly. Though it seemed like a small thing, it made a big difference in building trust between them. Paula felt like Phil was attending to her needs more and that he really cared about taking care of their home together.

A request is an *invitation* to cooperate, not a demand. Ask for what you want in a clear and respectful way. Talk to each other as though you are partners seeking to accomplish the same goal; after all, you are. When you have the ability to generate new options together, you will find that you and your partner are cooperating and creating—not just compromising.

Exercise: Asking for What You Need

Start this exercise individually and then complete it with your partner.

THINK:	Think about what it is you might ask your partner to do that, if accomplished, would make you happier in your relationship.
DO:	Make a list of three things that you would like your partner to do. Make sure that at least one of your requests is neither too easy or so difficult that your partner might decline fulfilling it.
	Make one request of your partner each day, and have your partner make one request of you. Repeat the request to make sure both parties understand it completely. Practice accepting, declining or making counteroffers to your requests.
SHARE:	Talk about what it feels like to make requests of each other. What does it feel like to receive what you ask for? What does it feel like not to get what you ask for?

Rita and Chad were asked to do the above exercise by their marriage counselor. They had been married only a few months but went to get some counseling because Rita was feeling more and more resentful of Chad for not helping out around the house and with other chores. The first week they tried this exercise, they found out that Chad was not helping in part because he felt that

Rita was not interested in what was going on with him at work. *If she is not listening to me,* he thought, *why should I listen to her?* The exercise also demonstrated that they both had things they wanted to ask for but they did not feel comfortable making requests. Once they saw that they *both* had a wish list, it seemed more fair to make requests. In the second week they realized they did not have to hold back from asking for something. For instance, Chad shared that he wanted Rita to stay in bed with him longer in the morning on weekends. Rita shared that she wanted him to compliment her on how she looked every day, not just once in a while. They also realized that just because they asked for something or were asked for something, they did not have to agree to fulfill the request. They could just listen and counteroffer. They began to put aside a little time each week to do this exercise to make sure they were hearing and being heard. They found that the resentment they had disappeared.

Celebration—The Victory Dance

One of the best things about being on a team is celebrating your victories together. When you win as a team, it is not just *what* you have won; it is *how* you did it. Your success may often seem small or may happen in the middle of many other things you are doing. Stop and celebrate it, anyway, in any manner that feels appropriate to you—go out for a special dinner, throw a party or buy a present for yourselves together. This is your victory dance. It is a victory over individualism and separateness and an expression of yourselves as Couple.

Kyle and Portia had wanted to have a child since they were first married six years ago. They had suffered through two miscarriages and years of trying to get pregnant without success. Kyle was very supportive of Portia but did not know how to help. She was not sure what to tell him. She often felt that not having a child was her fault, although he never said that. They went to see another fertility specialist, who made some suggestions about what they might do. "For one thing," he said, "you will have to help each other with this. If you work together, you can win." They had never really considered conceiving as something to win, as a game to play as a team.

Some of the doctor's suggestions pertained to their preparations for lovemaking and their actual performance. They had to select a particular time of day to make love. This required some cooperation in scheduling. They had to purchase some items to help them stay in certain sexual positions for longer periods of time. They would meet and have a little "huddle" before they began. Afterward they would discuss how it went and certainly share some laughter. But they were very dedicated to their mission. When Portia became pregnant and delivered a healthy baby boy, they really felt it was a team accomplishment all the way through. They were also grateful to the doctor for coaching them. Even though they were very busy with the new baby, they decided to have a small party one Sunday afternoon, and they invited the doctor and a few close couples they knew. The party was not just to celebrate the baby, they said; it was to celebrate the fact that they had won the game as a team.

The Power of Cooperation

Cooperation allows couples to pool their resources and capitalize on their strengths. It also builds the capacity to trust each other and to encourage each other to persevere and produce results. Once commitment is unquestioned, practicing cooperation helps to keep Couple going. It feels great to be in a powerful partnership, to be powerful as partners and to experience the sense of power that results when goals are achieved through cooperation. With cooperation, you can take on anything together, knowing that you can do it and supporting each other in making it work. If cooperation is added to the mix, what may have started out as incompatibilities between partners may turn out to be diversity and versatility in the service of your lifelong love.

Look into your own life and pinpoint areas where you have been operating on your own so far that might benefit from cooperation with your partner. Imagine what it would be like to have a teammate working with you in all these areas. Even though particular activities may be simple or boring, doing them together can be a powerful and even fun experience. Lifelong love needs to be fun, and it can be when you cooperate.

CHAPTER FIVE

Communication:

The Third Step toward Lifelong Love

"You cannot find the new words
if you do not shatter the old words."
—C. G. Jung, *The Red Book*

One of the most common responses we hear when we ask couples to name the major difficulty in their relationship is, "We need to learn to communicate better." One or both of you may feel that you are not heard, noticed, appreciated or understood well enough. That may be the case, and improving your communication is definitely important. However, just learning new communication skills may not be sufficient to turn things around. While useful in many respects, communicating your feelings does not usually, in and of itself, solve the problem. It is like putting the cart before the horse.

In fact, in some cases, communicating negative feelings, even in a controlled setting, such as a counseling session, could make things worse. Research by Doss, Jones and Christensen has shown that some of the common interactions fostered in marital therapy, such as arguing and fighting, may actually lead to an increase in the types of problems for which the couples originally sought help. In the name of "better communication," couples often attack, blame, berate and hurt each other, serving only to reinforce the battle lines between them. You need to be careful about what you say, because words can tear down as easily as they can build up.

Communication is the third of the Four C's of Couple Power, not the first, as you might think it would be, for a very good reason. The underlying support structures in a relationship must be built and strengthened first as a basis for good and clear communication. Once the foundation of a commitment is established and the skills of cooperation have been developed, then training in effective communication can be very powerful. Without a commitment to working on your relationship, there can be no real cooperation. And without cooperation, there is little lasting value in communication. For communication to be useful and successful, you and your partner must commit to communicate responsibly, and you must stick with the process as a team until you both feel you have reached a mutual goal. Good communication now becomes the vehicle for reaping the fruits of the relationship.

The negativity of "the old words," as Carl Jung called them in the quotation above, must be transformed before "the new words" can be found and used to communicate effectively. This chapter explores specific communication practices, techniques and actions for accomplishing this paradigm shift and for maintaining lifelong love. The techniques presented here apply to all the couple personality types described in Chapter Two, regardless of age, marital status, gender, sexual orientation, ethnicity or anything else.

Responsible Speaking

Communication is not something that just happens to us. It comes from the action of *giving* and *joining*. When communicating is done responsibly, you and your partner will see yourselves as active agents, instead of passive participants reacting to the control exerted by the other person. When you operate in this way, you build trust and create a spirit of giving, not blaming. You join together as a team to work on your problems and devise creative solutions. The objective is to talk *to* each other, not *at* each other, so that both partners are completely understood. That kind of understanding is truly a gift. It is an opportunity to share something that maintains lifelong love.

Communicating with this kind of intention fits the dictionary definition of the word *responsible*—"to be accountable for the performance or discharge of duty or trust; able to answer for one's behavior; trustworthy." You may recognize in this definition characteristics of the Dynamic Couple, described earlier, who continually create new possibilities through their communication. Dynamic Couples are not victims of their circumstances but the directors of the fate of their relationship. They don't just automatically react to situations; they stop, cull from their own experiences and then choose how to respond. One of the key ways to do this is through the responsible use of language—both listening and speaking. When this is missing, as it often is in interactions of the three common couple personality types, problems can occur.

Janet and Donald, a Traditional Couple with one child and currently separated, discovered this the hard way. They had been married for ten years, and their lives had become separate in many ways, as Janet worked long hours in her law practice and

Donald, an out-of-work architect, made new friends outside their relationship. Janet started individual therapy with Phyllis and then asked her to conduct a joint therapy session for her and Donald to help them communicate their feelings and intentions to each other. They met for one session, but as they began to argue and defend themselves, it quickly became clear that neither commitment nor cooperation had been established in their relationship. Feelings and expressions of anger and hurt were escalating. Phyllis pointed this out and stopped them from communicating in such a negative manner. Only if they would both agree to work on their commitment to their relationship, Phyllis said, could they continue productively. Donald admitted that he did not want to do that, so communication about their marriage could no longer be effective at this point. After their many months of struggling, they began talking about divorce. At least they were now both being responsible for their listening and speaking and could make an informed decision. Janet now felt like she was an active agent in her life, rather than a victim of her circumstances, waiting for her husband or her therapist to fix things. Donald stopped giving Janet mixed messages and started moving on with his life.

Accepting the kind of responsibility that is required for effective communication is usually easier said than done. Our culture and our language are not set up to support us in taking responsibility for maintaining lifelong relationships. Rather, having been taken care of from birth to young adulthood, we often expect our partner or spouse to take over the role of our parents. That arrangement may work well for a time, but rarely succeeds in the long run. And the language you learned from the time you began to talk is likely not that of responsible speaking. When conflict strikes, most of us resort to blaming someone else. We use the word *you* to point a finger at the other person, rather than taking responsibility for our own feelings and actions by using the word *I*. "You made me angry" may be your explanation of what happened, but no one can really *make* us feel anything. Saying "I feel angry when you do that" is a much more accurate statement, and one that allows you to be more in control of your reactions and your life.

Another simple way to take responsibility for how you communicate with your partner is to use the word *we* rather than *I*. The couple proclamation you made likely includes the word *we*, and as you say it aloud daily, you will begin to think in terms of *we*. You can use *we* to emphasize joint responsibility for what is going on in your relationship, even when it may seem awkward. To say "We are angry," even when only one of you appears to feel that way, may help you to assume joint responsibility for a difficult situation. While it may feel uncomfortable to use *we* in this way, you may notice that you feel more generous and accepting toward each other when you do. By changing perspective and using Couple language, you sidestep blame and guilt, recognizing that no one person is at fault. Remember, it takes two to foxtrot or to cha-cha!

Exercise: Devoting a Day to *We*

Choose a day of the week or month to use only the word *we* when referring to yourself or your partner. This exercise may seem diffi-cult or silly. That's okay. Notice what you feel when you eliminate *I* from your speech and rely on *we*.

Nonverbal Communication

We are such a verbal culture that we often forget to pay attention to the significant nonverbal aspects of communication. It's not just what you say; it's how you say it. Nonverbal cues—like tone of voice, gestures, body movements, eye contact and, especially, touch—can communicate what we mean more powerfully than words, because we are often more affected by *how* something is said than by *what* is said. While threatening in some cultures, making eye contact in our culture conveys intimacy, openness and honesty, which are all useful qualities in communicating with your partner. Your partner may say "I love you" often, but you may still not believe it. But if an intimate tone of voice or eye contact or a special gesture or touch is added, your partner's proclamation of love may suddenly become much more believable.

All of these nonverbal communication behaviors are meaningful, but they are only really useful if you've made a commitment to your couple. Without a joint commitment to your relationship, nonverbal behaviors are likely to be ineffective and even destructive. A tone of sarcasm can be hurtful to one's partner, and overly aggressive touching, such as hitting or punching, is likely physical abuse and must be stopped. Sometimes professional consultation is needed in these cases. (See Chapter Nine for ways to receive help if you are in this situation.)

As long as it is not sarcastic or aggressive or otherwise negative, adding a nonverbal component to your couple proclamation, as mentioned earlier, will enhance the power of your communication. One couple with the proclamation "You are number one in my life" added the practice of holding hands, looking into each other's eyes, and then holding up their index fingers as an expression of being "number one." It always made them smile each time they did it.

Exercise: Adding a Nonverbal Element to Your Proclamations

Take a moment to look into each other's eyes and be silent together after saying your proclamation. Notice what you are feeling. Share with each other the level of intimacy you are experiencing between you now.

Exercise: Practicing Trust

Find a place where you both feel safe and try out a trust exercise, such as the "Blind Walk," in which one partner closes his or her eyes and is led silently on a walk, or the "Trust Fall," in which one person closes his or her eyes and falls backward into the other's arms. Switch roles and share your experiences with one another. You may notice feelings of fear and a sense of security when you do these exercises together.

Sex

The act of nonverbal communication that seems to bring up the most intense feelings, both positive and negative, is sex. This intensity often makes it difficult to talk about sex. In addition, our self-consciousness and even guilt about sex make speaking honestly and openly about it one of the most difficult undertakings in our culture. We hardly even have language to speak about it that is not medical, euphemistic or crude. Moreover, our inability to discuss sex openly is one of the greatest barriers to our sexual satisfaction. This discomfort often prevents partners from sharing their sexual desires and needs, even when they may have good communication in other areas. This situation does not usually improve over time. Once the partners reach middle age or have been married for many years, their sex life is likely to wane or become routine.

Helen and Michael, a Self-Focused Couple, had been married thirty years and hadn't had sex in more than two years. They came for therapy with Phyllis to see if they could rekindle this part of their relationship. Sex had become physically painful for Helen, even with medically prescribed creams and hormones. It had gotten to the point where they were both afraid to initiate sex—Helen for fear of it not working, and Michael out of fear of rejection. While in therapy they created the proclamation "Day by day in every way we are closer and closer" and began to talk about it all. Especially important for Helen was being able to share her feelings about being raped when she was eighteen years old and her anger about an affair Michael had had early on in their relationship.

As Michael listened to her, she began to feel his empathy and patience. They agreed to alter their busy schedules and make their relationship a priority. After several sessions of therapy, they went away for a romantic weekend. When they got back, they reported having a "sexually successful vacation," finding positives and humor in everything, including their "romantic dinner" of pizza and champagne in their hotel room because the gourmet restaurant they had planned to go to was closed. By the time they ended therapy, they were having regular "champagne and pizza" sex dates and were reciting their new proclamation, "The world is our oyster, and we are the cocktail sauce!"

Making a sexual relationship work is similar to creating a powerful couple proclamation. First of all, it is important to find private time and space to be together. You may want to include some special things to enhance your intimate encounter, like enjoyable scents and taste sensations. Then say your couple proclamation together, looking into each other's eyes, before you make love. Feel the power of your closeness and the intimacy of your gaze. Feel the positive connection of your couple proclamation.

You can further enhance your nonverbal physical experience by simply touching and appreciating each other's bodies. Without talking, use your hands to adjust the intensity and placement of your partner's touch. It is often easier to communicate your desires this way, especially if it is hard for one or both of you to express what you want verbally. You may find it easier to talk about it after indicating what you like and dislike nonverbally first. Another nonverbal intimate activity you can do is taking a shower or bath together. Take turns washing each other and sharing this intimate physical space together. Notice how this feels, and talk about it later. Couples are generally assigned these activities in the initial part of a sex therapy program. You might want to consult a therapist about going through such a program if you feel that you need more help in this area. (See Chapter Nine.) In any case, take some time to develop the sexual part of your life. It is an important aspect of lifelong love. Like any physical muscle, if you don't exercise it, it weakens. As they say, use it or lose it!

Exercise: Enhancing Your Sexual Relationship

Choose a nonverbal sexual activity to do together, such as messaging or taking a shower or bath. Discuss your experience afterward.

Laughter

Other than having sex, one of the best nonverbal things you and your partner can do together is laugh with each other. Seeing the humor in our own behavior and being able to laugh at ourselves are powerful tools for communication. If we take ourselves too seriously, we run the risk of getting stuck. Be careful not to create humor at the expense of your partner, however. The Dynamic Couple is able to laugh *with* each other, not at each other.

It was most certainly our sense of humor that rescued us from a huge argument many years ago. We were in the second week of a rigorous diet together that required eating only certain foods at specific times. This night it was broccoli, and Peter was late bringing it home from the grocery store. Phyllis was famished and couldn't reach Peter (before the days of cell phones). When he walked in the house one hour later, Phyllis was ready to bite his head off. He gave her the broccoli to cook, and she was so mad, she threw it at him. Peter was shocked and annoyed and picked up the phone book and threw it at her. It fell into the dog bowl, and the dogs started barking. Soon we were laughing at ourselves and the situation. We hugged each other and vowed to find another way to deal with our dieting and nutritional goals that was less stressful on our relationship, but it was quite a funny scene that we will never forget.

Responsible listening

Responsible speaking is crucial to the functioning of a Dynamic Couple. Communication is a two-way street, however, that involves listening as well as speaking. There is so much pressure in our media-driven culture to say the right thing that we don't give enough attention to *hearing* what was said. Though relatively simple to do, listening is not a very well developed skill for most people. In fact, most people remember only a small percentage of what is said in any situation. With our partners, that may be partly because we are just waiting our turn to get into the act and say what we want to say; or we may be too busy feeling defensive to focus on what is being said. A simple rule of thumb that works in almost all situations with your partner is to listen first and speak next.

The key to communicating effectively is "responsible listening." Like responsible speaking, responsible listening requires being fully committed to work on the relationship and to cooperate with each other for the mutual benefit of the couple. It means taking responsibility to be aware of your own part in whatever the issue is, not just listening for what's wrong with your partner. This takes being open to hearing your partner's experience respectfully, without projecting onto him or her your own feelings, interpretations or expectations. As Socrates said centuries ago, first "know thyself."

Responsible listening also means being fully present and attentive when your partner is speaking, committing to know and understand fully his or her thoughts and feelings. This is consistent with the description of communication mentioned earlier as coming from the "action of giving." It is truly a gift to be listened to attentively. It may feel almost like a sacred act, like the reciting of one of the most important Hebrew prayers, the *Shema,* one meaning of which is "listen." Listening is also inherent in the traditional marriage vow to "love, honor and obey," since a definition of *obey* is "to lend an ear to." While most of us certainly don't want to "obey" our partner, we can recognize that the root of "to obey" is linked to the words "to hear" and can generously give the gift of listening to each other.

Sometimes responsible listening is easier said than done, however. We have experienced this in our own relationship. Peter likes to talk about his day as soon as he gets home from work, but Phyllis isn't always in the mood to hear him vent about everything that happened, and she wants to have a chance to share some feelings about her own day. In order to work out our differences so that our time together is mutually satisfying, we agreed to do a few simple exercises, like those described below.

Exercise: "Five and Five"

In this exercise you and your partner agree to spend ten minutes listening to each other without interrupting or reacting, verbally or nonverbally. You each are allotted exactly five minutes. You may want to set a timer to ensure you both get a full five minutes. Decide who will go first, and then switch. After doing this listening exercise, you may notice, as we did, that you both feel more relaxed and ready to listen to each other. More space has been created by the gift of listening and knowing that you will both have time for some needed release.

As with all the exercises suggested here, say your couple proclamation together before commencing. You might think of it as saying a prayer or blessing before an important meeting or gathering. It shows that we respect what we are about to do or say and consider it important.

Exercise: Feedback

In this exercise one partner simply requests that the other listen with full awareness, without judging or analyzing what is said. The listener then repeats what was said, and the speaker listens to make sure that s/he was completely understood. Keep going until you both agree that the communication is complete and the speaker has a sense of being heard. You will both know when that has happened: you will feel that a wonderful gift has been given and received—the gift of listening. How many times do we really feel completely heard? The experience of it can be healing in and of itself, and frequently it staves off an argument or conflict.

Exercise: Checking It Out

This exercise is designed to check out your assumptions about what your partner is thinking or feeling. Couples, especially those who have been together a long time, tend to assume that they know each other's thoughts and feelings, but frequently this kind of mind reading is off the mark. Even if it is just a little off base, it can make a big difference in the way you relate. Ask your partner for permission to "check his or her mind about something," and if it is all right with your partner, follow the instructions below. If it is not okay at the moment, select a time to do this within the next twenty-four hours.

THINK:	Identify an issue or situation that is significant in your relationship at the moment. What are you assuming your partner thinks or feels about the situation or issue?
DO:	Tell your partner what you think s/he is thinking or feeling about this issue or situation. Then ask what percentage of your assumption, between 0 and 100 percent, is correct. If it is less than 100 percent correct, ask your partner to tell you where you erred, and then repeat back your partner's thoughts on the matter, as in the feedback practice above. Keep going until your partner

feels completely understood. There is no getting to
a right or wrong answer, just working together for
clarity and resolution.

SHARE: What did it feel like for each of you to examine your
assumptions in this way? What did you find out that
you didn't know before?

A good example of how to use the "Checking It Out" exercise is
provided by Scott and Marilyn, a Traditional Couple, who had been
married for twenty-five years. Scott was the head of a large company, and Marilyn felt like the "backup" person for him and the
family. After their kids left for college, their relationship seemed
to fall apart. They came for counseling with Phyllis when they
stopped having fun together and started arguing about almost
everything. They couldn't even agree on saying their proclamation
and stopped reciting it regularly. It came out in a therapy session
that Scott felt like Marilyn was making fun of the proclamation
when they said it. There was something about how she said it, he
explained. They became aware of the power of their nonverbal
communication and did the "Checking It Out" exercise to explore
further what was going on. Scott checked out his observation
about the proclamation with Marilyn, and she said that it was only
10 percent correct. She admitted that she had been making fun of
the proclamation a bit when they recited it, but that 90 percent of
this had to do with the awkwardness she felt about saying it. As
a result of sharing these feelings, they changed their proclamation
to "We have fun exploring the world together," which they both felt
more comfortable with, and they started saying it on a daily basis.

Managing Conflict

A crucial time to use responsible speaking and listening is when managing the conflicts that come up in your relationship. Conflict is a natural occurrence in relationships. It is necessary and even desirable for keeping a Dynamic Couple relationship alive and growing. Dealt with responsibly, conflict is an opportunity to get some important issues resolved. Without conflict, your relationship may become stuck and boring. No conflict being expressed may also be a sign that someone is suppressing their feelings and building up resentment, which will explode sometime in the future, leading to emotional and physical difficulties. The mind-body connection is a powerful one and can be helpful or harmful, depending on the situation. If ignored, stored-up negative feelings can threaten your health and the quality, if not the survival, of your relationship. Many people are afraid of conflict and avoid it, however.

You and/or your partner may be one of those who avoid facing problems in your relationship for fear of losing the other person or of being hurt emotionally, economically or even physically. Certainly, you must ensure your safety and get professional help if you are being physically abused. (See Chapter Nine.) In most cases, however, there is a different cost for "playing it safe"—losing intimacy, honesty, joy and satisfaction in your relationship. Communicating about conflict is an opportunity to create new methods for meeting both of your needs, taking you to a more powerful level of functioning.

Lifelong love does not grow naturally. Like a garden, it needs weeding and pruning in order to flourish. Without giving attention to communicating responsibly to manage conflict, that is, the "weeds" of a relationship, the garden will become overgrown, and the fruit will wither and die. Weeds grow naturally; lifelong love, like a flourishing garden, takes committed action. Here are some actions you might want to take when dealing with your own disagreements.

State your couple proclamation

Our most essential "gardening tool" for managing conflict is the couple proclamation. You never want to go into the weeds without it. You are likely to get hurt by the sharp thorns on the stems if you don't use it. So once you have identified an area of conflict that you want to discuss together, begin by stating your couple proclamation either by yourself or with each other. No matter how upset you are, don't go any further in your communication until you have done this. Otherwise, you may do more harm than good with your sharing, creating a block to any progress. Saying your proclamation allows you to stay focused on the commitment you have made to your relationship, and prevents you from losing sight of what you value in it. Your commitment is the strong foundation for what you are working on together; without it, it's like building on sand. So say your couple proclamation in the face of conflict to keep the foundation for lifelong love stable and secure.

Exercise: Saying Your Proclamation When Facing Conflict

Recall your couple proclamation and open your heart to it—even for a second. That is where you started, and it is the best place to come from. It keeps you from dwelling on your pain in the past and becoming a victim of it, and it allows you to focus on what's possible for the future. Do this exercise by yourself when you get upset, and together before you begin discussing an issue with your partner.

Accept negative feelings
and take responsibility for them

Perhaps the most difficult and problematic part of dealing with conflict is acknowledging any negative feelings you may have toward your partner, such as anger or jealousy. You may be concerned about your own level of control or your partner's reaction to your feelings, or you may be embarrassed to admit that you feel jealous or insecure. Connecting with your negative feelings is crucial, however, for healing them and managing conflict with your partner. If you deny your negative feelings or try to avoid dealing with them, you may hang on to them and they may only get worse.

Once you become aware of your pain, spend some time on your own to take responsibility for your feelings before sharing them. It is like responsible listening for your own experience. Begin by saying your couple proclamation to yourself, as suggested in the exercise above. Then ask yourself some questions: Can I see my own part in the conflict? Can I have some compassion for my partner? Do I see some possibility for a resolution? You may want to write down your answers or share them with a confidant. Be careful about sharing too much with a friend or confidant, however, rather than your spouse. While it may feel supportive, you risk reducing the intimacy you have with your partner.

Difficult as it might have been to do, the wife of one couple used this approach with remarkable results. After several sessions of marital therapy with Phyllis, Lynette and Doug, a Self-Focused Couple, who had been married about six years and had two busy careers and no children, decided to separate. Doug moved to another city, and Lynette stayed in weekly therapy with Phyllis, sometimes reluctantly. Lynette said, "Therapy helped me to be accountable for the contributions I was making to our failing marriage and to be honest about everything that was going on—

to stop playing games and grow up! No one ever took me to task about this before, and I was firmly rooted in blaming Doug for everything." A year after what they called "the cold war" or "the divorce years," they sent Phyllis a birth announcement about their new baby boy. They wrote in it, "If we hadn't gone through the conflict and therapy, we wouldn't be as strong as we are today. Our marriage is now honest, open, fulfilling and joyous because of it all. We enjoy each other so much and have a beautiful family. Thank you!"

Clearing it up

After you have done this self-reflection, if you are still upset, let your partner know that you want to discuss the area of conflict. Don't wait too long to do this, because when you hang on to your negative feelings, you build up resentments that will undermine your relationship. Unexpressed feelings from the past affect our relationships in the present, so it is important to get these feelings cleared up so you can stop focusing on the hurt and concentrate on fulfilling what you want for your relationship now. The Dalai Lama often says that we may not be able to avoid pain, but we don't need to add suffering on top of it.

When it comes time to discuss the matter, keep an open mind, and listen to what your partner has to say as much as possible. If the going gets rough, you may need to take a "time-out" for a few minutes to cool off and do some self-reflection. Then resume your discussion. This cooling off is a restraint, not a tool of suppression. Self-restraint will help you both be more responsible about your speaking and listening. It is important that both of you feel safe enough to have a "fair fight." Without that atmosphere of safety, no communication techniques will work, even if you know them perfectly. If you are responsible about how you argue, you can avoid destructive escalation, while still working on resolving the conflict. As the great Indian philosopher Mahatma Gandhi said, "A really self-restrained person grows every day from strength to strength and from peace to more peace. The very first step in self-restraint is the restraint of thoughts. Understand your limitations and do only as much as you can."

One thing you can always do to get on the right track, as mentioned above, is say your couple proclamation; recite it together after you have cooled off and before you get into working on the conflict again. You may feel overwhelmed at the time, but if you name it and proclaim it, you can tame it. If you say your couple proclamation when working on a conflict, no matter how upset you are, you are bound to see it as a demonstration of the level of commitment you have to your couple. And if one or both of you raise your voice, you might be more apt to interpret it as an expression of caring, commitment and passion for your relationship, rather than an attack or criticism, if you have recited your couple proclamation.

Another way to create an atmosphere of safety and caring for resolving conflict is to do a structured exercise with rules for having a fair fight, as in the exercise below. You could also do some of the simple listening exercises mentioned above, or you might want to try the "Clearing It Up" exercise described here, which is modeled after George Bach's Fair-Fight Training Program (1971).

Exercise: Clearing It Up

THINK: Each of you think of some unresolved issue or conflict you have with your partner. You may start with whoever has the most "urgent business," or just choose who will go first.

DO:	Begin by selecting a safe place and a good time for the discussion. The partner who has the most urgent business should take the lead in dealing with these logistics. If there is not a good time at the moment, the discussion should be held within the next two days. To begin the discussion, the speaker describes the issue, sticking to the facts without making any accusations, and includes how s/he felt about the issue then and now. The listener feeds back the speaker's account until the speaker is satisfied that s/he has been heard. Then the listener asks, "What was it about what I did that you found hardest to take?" The speaker shares what s/he felt most hurt or angry about, and the listener repeats that back. End by thanking each other for sharing and listening.
SHARE:	How do you both feel now? Share with each other what difference doing this exercise may make for your couple in the future.

Marilyn asked her husband, Scott, to do this exercise after they came back from a shopping trip during which Scott bought an expensive television without asking for her input. Being part of a Traditional Couple, Marilyn was not used to being consulted about major purchases that Scott intended to make. This time, however, rather than holding on to her resentment over this, she informed him that she had some unfinished business to discuss with him. They did the "Clearing It Up" exercise, and she told him that the hardest part of being left out of the decision making was feeling devalued. This led them to examine their proclamation "We value our couple" more carefully and begin to work in their therapy on consulting with each other more.

Acknowledge positive feelings

Expressing positive feelings to each other is just as important as sharing the negative ones. This fosters intimacy during the high points of your life together and strengthens your relationship during the low points. A key element in communicating positive feelings to your partner is *acknowledgment*, the practice of noticing and appreciating something positive that one of you has said or done. Acknowledgment is not an expensive commodity, but we are often stingy with it. That is a sad state of affairs, especially since experts maintain that this simple act of positive attention is what people need most—even more than expressions of love—to function well. In fact, happy couples have been shown to make positive statements to each other five times more often than unhappy couples.

The fact is that the more you give acknowledgment, the more you get back; and what you don't reinforce will disappear. Basic principles of behavioral psychology demonstrate clearly that rewarding positive behavior is much more effective than punishment or trying to change unwanted behavior. Actions that are rewarded are likely to recur more often. Thus, it is helpful to acknowledge frequently the things your partner does that you like and that you might normally take for granted, such as cooking dinner, taking care of a sick child or pet, mowing the lawn, doing the laundry and so on. This kind of appreciation is what close friends share with each other. Why not treat our partners at least as nicely as we treat our friends?

What adds uniqueness to your relationship with your partner, and enables your relationship to transcend a friendship, is the building block of lifelong love—the couple as an entity. So it is important to realize how an acknowledgment of either partner includes an appreciation of the couple as a whole. If you get or seek acknowledgment for something you did without recognizing how that accomplishment was made possible in part by your relationship, it will not have much lasting value for Couple. For example, if your partner acknowledges you for getting a raise, be sure to also appreciate your partner's contribution in supporting you and/or the family to help make that possible. Scott did this with Marilyn after she told him how proud she was of him for getting a promotion. He expressed his appreciation to her for making it possible by taking such good care of their home every day. This served to reinforce their proclamation "We value our couple" and increased their trust in the power of their relationship. So the emphasis is on acknowledging not just what you *did* but also how *being* Couple, your commitment and vision for lifelong love, made that accomplishment possible.

To be truly effective, an acknowledgment must be fully experienced by both the speaker and the listener. Often we do not communicate our appreciation specifically and meaningfully enough. If you are sick and your partner brings you breakfast in bed, your acknowledgment means a lot more if you say, "I really appreciate your bringing me my breakfast," than if you just say, "Thank you." Also, make sure that you begin by saying, "I appreciate…" or "I acknowledge you for…," rather than "I want to…" or "I would like to acknowledge you for…." The first two phrases make for a more powerful statement; the extra words in the last two dilute the impact of your acknowledgment. Don't just *want* to do it, *do* it.

It is also important to note that as much as we want to be recognized for something we did, we often have a hard time accepting praise, no matter how clearly it is given. You may prevent yourself from fully experiencing the act of recognition out of embarrassment or pent-up resentment over not having been acknowledged in the past. It is up to you as the receiver of praise to let it sink in and let your partner know his or her message has been truly heard. Also, you may want to request acknowledgment for something you did that went unrecognized by your partner. The appreciation is no less valuable if you ask for it. Finally, stop and notice how your partner appears to you once you have shared an acknowledgment. You will likely see each other in a more positive light than before. It may also be easier to discuss other matters and express opinions after giving or receiving some appreciation. That is the power of praise.

Exercise: Sharing Praise

Start keeping a list of things you appreciate about your partner and your relationship. Then begin and end each day for at least a week by sharing praise and acknowledging the things each of you has accomplished or contributed to your relationship.

Lynette and Doug, the Self-Focused Couple described earlier, did this exercise and shared the things they loved about each other every day for a week. They said, "Even on the days when we had nothing nice to say, we still managed to find something kind to share, and it reminded us of what attracted us to each other in the first place."

Exercise: Accentuating the Positive

Make a list of some of the negative things you cleared up and burn or shred the list. Do the "Clearing It Up" exercise, but this time share some positive "unfinished business." Ask your partner, "What was it about what I said/did that you particularly liked?" Repeat your partner's response to make sure you heard it correctly.

Renaming Negatives as Positives

Another way to stay positive when dealing with difficult issues is to use the power of language to rename or reframe negative statements or situations as positive intentions and possibilities. The classic example is to see the glass as half full rather than half empty. If one or both of you raise your voice during a disagreement, for example, you can rename this "attack" or "criticism" as an expression of caring, commitment and passion for your relationship. Your frustration is then a matter of a failure of Couple, rather than the failure of either individual. There is pain because there is a commitment to your relationship. Sometimes the more we care, the more we hurt. This perspective allows you to cooperate in finding solutions to the problem rather than determining who is at fault, which doesn't really get you anywhere. Then you can reframe your complaints as requests or acknowledgments, focusing on making progress instead of describing what's wrong. For example, even though Marilyn was angry that Scott came home late for dinner one night, she turned her complaint into praise, acknowledging him for how hard he was working for their family and for calling ahead to let her know. She also requested that they work out a better arrangement in the future, and they began working together on a schedule that respected each of their opinions and needs.

Exercise: Giving a Negative a Positive Name

When a negative situation comes up, create several different names for the situation that allow you to see it more positively.

Even changing one word in a sentence can help transform your experience of conflict from a negative into something positive or, at least, open up the possibility. That one word is *but*. It is a small word, and it has a lot of power, almost always as a downer. For example, Jane and Don, a couple in their sixties, went on vacation on their new boat together. Don's fishing line got tangled, and he got upset. Jane said, "I could have had a good time, but you got so angry." She was about to ruin the whole day for both of them, until she stopped herself and changed the *but* in her sentence to *and*. She realized she had a choice about it and was able to allow Don to let off steam and to allow herself to go on and have fun. They both enjoyed the rest of the day and the vacation, which wouldn't have happened otherwise.

Exercise: Getting Rid of *But*

Notice when you use the word *but* when talking to or about each other. When you catch yourself or your partner uttering *but*, change the word to *and*. Notice what your relationship is like without *but* in it and share your observations with each other.

You can do more than change just one word; you can change the whole name of a project or a situation you feel negatively about to something more positive. We did that when we were in the process of reorganizing and cleaning up our house for a large event. After several days of working on our project, we started arguing and feeling discouraged about the whole thing. Then we changed our perspective, no longer thinking about the project as chores each of us had to complete but as our mission to see how beautiful the house could look. We gave the project a name, "House Beautiful," and put it at the top of a chart we made of the various areas we wanted to beautify. Suddenly we started feeling excited about working together on the house, rather than blaming each other for not getting it done—and we even had fun doing it. Giving our project a new name breathed new energy into it. Rather than staying upset and hoping that the situation would change, we were able to create new possibilities just by using new language.

The Written Word

The written word is a powerful tool and can be used both individually and by you and your partner together to communicate your feelings in a variety of ways.

Journaling

Writing down your feelings in a personal journal can be a very effective way to clarify your own thinking and, consequently, be more responsible when you speak to your partner. Taking the time to write your thoughts down, and then reviewing them before you communicate with your partner, will help you to be more aware of your feelings and your own part in a conflict and will help to put things into perspective.

Exercise: Writing in a Journal

Buy a journal and practice writing in it for a few minutes every day, focusing on how you are feeling about your relationship. Jot down what you appreciated that day or the day before, note what was missing that would enhance your couple's vision, describe some things you might do differently and write down a request you may have for your partner. Continue doing this journaling as long as it is helpful.

The art of letter writing

Nowadays email is the preferred method of communication for many people, but keep in mind how easy it is to press that Send button. Once you've done so, your words are out there, not to be changed. Especially in times of conflict, be careful what you say to each other in emails.

The nearly forgotten art of letter writing may be more useful in these situations. You can take the time to think about what you want to say—and whether or not you want to send the letter. Writing a letter can be particularly helpful in resolving difficult issues that you have been working on for some time in your relationship. In thinking about the issues, you may come to see that you have some related unresolved issues with a parent or another important person from your past. Even if that person has passed on, you may want to write a letter to them first. While it may be difficult to do this, it is important to stay positive throughout the letter in order to get to a real state of resolution.

Exercise: Writing a Letter

Identify an unresolved issue in your relationship. Then write a letter to your partner or to someone from your past who is somehow connected to that issue. Start by acknowledging all the things that person has contributed to your life, leaving out any complaints. Then share your responsibility for how the relationship is, and leave out the other person's part for now. Next, request what you want from the person and note what you will do for the relationship. End with a statement of acceptance of the other person for who they are, even if you don't like what they did. You don't have to agree with the person to communicate that you accept them.

Marilyn and Scott had been feeling very discouraged about their relationship for several weeks, even to the point of considering divorce. When talking about her childhood during one of their therapy sessions with Phyllis, Marilyn said that she "didn't have a father." The fact was that he had died when she was nine years old, and she had never completed grieving his death. At Phyllis's suggestion and with Scott's support, Marilyn wrote a letter to her father, following the guidelines described above. When they came to their therapy session the next week, Marilyn and Scott were holding hands and reported that things were going much better. She read her letter out loud and cried. Scott reached over and hugged her. She was then able to say goodbye to her father and say hello to her husband in a new way—not as a substitute father figure, but as a husband who loved her.

Greeting cards and love notes

It's no accident that greeting cards are a multimillion-dollar business. There is something very powerful and moving about reading positive sentiments from people we love and who love us. Never underestimate the impact of some well-chosen words that express your affection. Poets know that; greeting card companies know that. You can make use of your own language to enrich and maintain the lifelong love in your couple. Even if you just add a few words or sentences of your own to the bottom of a greeting card message, it makes the message more personal and meaningful.

There is something special about receiving something that your partner has taken the time to write and send to you. It says, "I've been thinking about you in a special way," whether it be from close by or far away. Especially nice are little love notes or letters that you leave around the house or in surprise places, such as the car, the office, a suitcase or a lunch box.

Exercise: Writing Love Notes

Write some love notes to your partner. Leave them in special places, or hide them under a pillow to find later or in a place you reveal when you call home. You may also want to write a longer love letter and mail it to your partner—perhaps while you are away on a trip.

By now you should have an ample supply of tools for effective communication. Don't get stuck in your disagreements. Life is too short. Instead speak and listen responsibly. Celebrate your accomplishments along the way. Get a babysitter, go out to dinner, make a toast to your couple and go dancing. Remember, the important thing is knowing not just *what* to do but *when* to do it. As long as commitment, cooperation and communication are present, you are ready to go on to the next step, the fourth of the Four C's of Couple Power—community.

CHAPTER SIX

Community:

The Fourth Step toward Lifelong Love

"In and through community lies the salvation of the world."
—M. Scott Peck, *The Different Drum*

Commitment, cooperation and communication are the essential building blocks of lifelong love, but the fourth and final C in the formula is what ties it all together and, when achieved, maintains a truly rewarding and satisfying relationship. This final step is what we call *community*. In this chapter we'll show you the value of having a community to support and enhance your couple.

Community for Couples

Many couples start out together doing well. The two partners may seek out their own space, away from the influences of family or friends. For them, their time as a couple is special, and they enjoy doing things as a twosome. They may have friends they still hang out with on a regular basis, but there is a pull for them to spend some time establishing their own identity as a couple. For many couples, the first years seem to go the best. It is a time of curiosity and exploration. After a while, however, the two partners may begin to struggle and experience internal stress or the negative effects of outside stressors. External pressures from work and careers, financial setbacks and familial concerns may begin to gnaw at the fabric of the relationship. When this occurs, some couples try to stick it out, hoping that more money, better jobs, a new place to live or having children will make things better. They may proceed this way for a few years or even decades.

For some couples, this is the time when they consider getting counseling or coaching. They may reach out to clergy, spiritual guides, therapists and the like. First attempts to get outside support or treatment are often successful in the short run. Just taking the step to patch up the relationship is an expression of commitment to it. The counseling might include exercises in remembering previous positive feelings or working on cooperation and communication skills. When treatment or enrichment efforts are completed, however, couples often return to the same isolated environment and experience their difficulties all over again, sinking back into the situation they were in before they sought help. They might have felt contentment when they completed their work in therapy, but it is often very difficult for them to sustain their success over time.

Allison and Ted met in college and got married a few years after graduation. They were a very social couple, often entertaining friends and other couples at home, and organizing group outings to the beach or the mountains. They went out with other couples on a weekly basis. At these gatherings, regardless of the activity or the place, the men usually spent a lot of time watching or talking about sports or discussing work, and the women drank wine and complained about their husbands. There was talk about relationships, but it usually involved gossip or expressions of dissatisfaction.

Allison and Ted had been struggling for a few years with their own relationship and with raising their two sons. They began marital therapy with Peter and benefited greatly from the sessions for a year. Near the end of their treatment, they reported to Peter that at a recent social event, their friends asked about their relationship, and they told them how great it was, how they felt a deeper commitment and were communicating more effectively. They said that their friends seemed almost "disappointed" that they would not join them in complaining anymore. Allison and Ted said they felt like they were losing some of their best friends because they had lost some of what they had in common. They liked what was happening in their relationship but didn't have anyone to share it with. "No one," they said, "seemed to want things to be better." They felt discouraged. It was such a downer to be with the friends they routinely socialized with, and they didn't have many other friends outside that circle.

Peter gave them the assignment to meet a new couple together during the following week. Allison went to pick up the children from child care a few days later and ran into another mother and father in the parking lot. She had seen them only from a distance before but noticed they had children who were about the same age. The parents seemed to be enjoying themselves, and Allison thought it would be interesting to meet them—especially in light of the assignment Peter had given them. She introduced herself, and they began talking. After a few minutes, Allison suggested that the four of them get together the following weekend. They agreed, and the two families got together at Ted and Allison's to swim in their pool and have dinner. At the end of the evening, they agreed to get together again and to even include some other families from child care.

Allison and Ted had not been getting any support in the outside world for the gains they had made in treatment. There weren't many happy couples around to emulate, and there was no manual on how to find other happy couples. They knew lots of discontented, unhappy couples, however. At first, Allison and Ted wondered where they would find positive models, but over time, they found that they needed only to look around for them on their own. They noticed they were attracted to happy couples, and that other happy couples seemed attracted to them.

As it turns out, just as it takes a village to raise a child, it takes a community to nourish and support your couple. Over the course of three decades of talking with people in relationships, we have come to see that the key to a joyful and durable relationship is a sense of community with others. When asked how they have stayed together for so long, stable couples say that they have close friends or family members in long-term relationships that they "hang around with." Some have chosen to retire to the same locations, while others plan annual trips together or rent a cottage together during vacations. Being in a community of couples provides ample opportunities for support and sharing, creating a powerful context for Couple. Without this support, a couple might feel isolated or overwhelmed, and the two partners might end up seeking help separately, outside their relationship, which may only discourage them more or even drive them apart.

How do you find or create a community of couples? Communities of couples already exist in a lot of places, and we need to make the effort to seek them out. There are a variety of ways to establish communities of couples, and many types of communities are possible.

The Need for Community

Humans have a long history of group and community behavior. Throughout evolutionary history, we have formed tribal groups or communities. Unlike some solitary animals, we have lived in families and extended family groups, villages and cities, not in small packs or alone. Even nomadic tribes have historically traveled together, rarely breaking apart or going off in smaller family units. In the twentieth century, however, small nuclear families developed, and these families gained mobility, moving away from the place of their origin for economic reasons, such as to secure employment or to seek other opportunities not available at home. It used to be that everything that we needed was in the village. Now people migrate all over the country and even the world, and they know much more about what exists beyond the borders of their town or city. In many couples, one or both partners have moved away from their extended families to begin their own family in a new location. This splintering of extended families often limits the support that parents and other family members can provide, whether that be helping out with child care or simply being a reassuring presence in a couple's life. This shift to a more mobile society did not preclude the need for or the existence of support systems. The nature of support simply needed to change.

One kind of community that has been preserved or is easily reestablished in a society that has become increasingly migratory is the community comprised of couples. When we speak of *couple communities,* we are not just describing groups of individuals, but what the couples provide to the communities and what the community provides the couples. You can be friends with a lot of couples who interact as a group, but this community may not be committed to the health and survival of its members' relationships. In the same way, you may belong to a community of your neighbors who are focused on hanging out and having fun, or on making your neighborhood safer, nicer or friendlier. The same is true for couple communities. You can be in groups *of* couples or groups *for* couples. So it is not just about community; it is about the needs that community fills. In other words, while being social, being with others, meets some of our natural social and human need for interaction, a group or community might also foster values we hold dear. It is important to point out that a healthy couple community is not a "place" to gain consensus about your perceptions of your partner's defects, but rather it is a place that adheres to the values of the larger commitment to Couple.

In our interviews over the years with couples who have been married a long time, we noticed a common theme: the need for couples to have other couples around them, couples who are also in lifelong relationships. Geraldine and Jared, a successful dual-career couple, described themselves as being very happy. They had never felt the need for marriage counseling or participated in a relationship-enrichment program. They certainly had faced some problems with family illness and had confronted challenges in parenting their four children. One child had a serious medical condition and some educational problems, and there were job stresses for both of them. How had they managed to stay so happy?

"We have a great group of couples we spend most of our time with," Geraldine revealed. "We go to the beach together every summer and are always talking to each other. Our children are about the same ages, and we can share just about anything with each other. When something goes wrong, we just call them up and ask them what they would do." Geraldine and Jared were actually describing a couple community they had developed over the years. The community was so close-knit that four of their best couple friends had been talking with them about buying houses near each other when they all retired in a few years.

The Benefits of Community

Many psychologists and sociologists have commented on the positive effects of communities. A dearth of communities and a lack of community participation have the opposite effect. In his book *Bowling Alone,* Robert Putnam speaks of the increasing trend of people going bowling but not joining bowling leagues. This lessening of social connection has been shown to be related to the experience of loneliness and to poor health. In fact, Putnam cites research that documents the positive relationship between well-being and integration at the community level. The more connected we are to our community, he says, the less likely we are to catch colds and suffer from strokes, depression and even cancer.

Community is the experience of identification with like-minded people. Community involvement serves to reinforce the notions that you are not alone and that support and understanding are available. Cultural, ethnic and religious communities foster the sense that you can be understood, even when the outside world may not seem to be understanding. Communities acknowledge and give credibility to experiences you have. Like coming home, a community can be a place to relax without the fear of being judged or singled out. We can all name a number of communities we live in and what those communities most value. Perhaps it is a language we speak, a cultural or ethnic heritage we share, or an experience we have in common, like serving in the military or being a cancer survivor. Yet we don't often think of or identify communities where the primary common value is to be in a lifelong relationship. Such communities do exist, however, or can be created when they are not present.

Communities of couples may include a large number of people or just a few. Some may meet regularly, gather only for special occasions or just get together on occasion. Regardless of these differences, they are a source of support to people in relationships and foster lifelong love.

The Types of Community

Generally speaking, communities may be "vertical," such as those consisting of extended families, parents and grandparents, or "horizontal," those involving our peers, our social network, neighborhood groups, religious groups, clubs and coaching organizations.

Vertical communities

We define *vertical communities* as those that cross generational lines and exist "up and down," from one generation through the next. Extended families often include three or four generations. Couples may feel support and encouragement in these vertical communities from great-grandparents, grandparents, parents and even children. Grandparents may give advice on how to communicate more clearly or may put an argument in perspective. They may offer their own experiences as examples or be an ongoing help and consultant to one or both members of the couple. The perspective they have gained over many years may help a couple assess the significance of what they are going through. They sometimes pass on strategies or wisdom that has served them well in the past.

Samantha and Drew just returned from their honeymoon. Samantha called her parents and told them that she was having some difficulty adjusting to her new last name, Collins. Friends that she talked to about it told her to just keep her own name, but she didn't feel comfortable with that either. She wanted to be known and connected as a couple by using the same last name. Samantha's mom, who had a hyphenated last name, listened sympathetically and told her how it had taken her some time to get accustomed to her name change, even with the hyphen. Her dad chimed in and suggested that she use her family name, Slaughter, as her middle name, at least for a while. Samantha told them she felt relieved after talking to them, realizing that it wasn't just about her name change but also about dealing with the loss of her nuclear family as it used to be. Talking with each other helped both generations deal with the transition.

In the first year of a relationship, parents can be very helpful in lending support and sharing recommendations for solving various problems. Conflicts invariably arise in new couples since the partners come from different families with different values and different practices. It is sometimes difficult for a couple to choose which practices to adhere to, but this creates an opportunity to do something entirely different from what has been done before, to expand how the vertical community sees things.

Kali and Dudley, guests on our cable television show about relationships, had been married about eight years. Their parents lived in different cities, and from the very beginning, deciding where to spend the winter holidays was a challenge. Kali's folks were part of a large family, and getting together at Christmas was a big deal. They lived a few days' drive away, and so traveling to visit them on Christmas Day precluded spending any time with Dudley's side of the family. When their girls were born, the first grandchildren on both sides of the family, everyone wanted to spend time with them. The couple felt a lot of pressure. It didn't satisfy everyone to alternate years, going to one set of in-laws for Thanksgiving and the other for Christmas, and there was not enough money to pay for both trips each year. Thanksgiving dinner seemed to be the most problematic. Dudley was an only child, and his parents were insistent that they spend this special time together. Added to the mix was the fact that both Kali and Dudley worked full-time and could not take off many days during the holidays. In addition, getting their young children ready to travel a long distance was quite a challenge, and it disrupted their child-care routine. It meant devoting more time and energy to the children when they got back from holiday trips.

Kali and Dudley spent a great deal of time arguing each year about where to go for the holidays. They each enjoyed being with their parents, and each favored their own side of the family. They agreed that their folks were very possessive and felt strongly about family traditions. Their vertical communities valued the tradition of family gatherings for celebrations and holidays. Kali and Dudley were tired out by the whole process every year and began to dread Thanksgiving. How could they honor the well-intended traditions of their families and not feel pressured, angry and resentful?

One night, when they were weighing the pros and cons of where to go for the holiday, they began to discuss what their family traditions were like for them growing up. Kali remembered that she was about four when Thanksgiving dinners began to be a big event in their household. Dudley also recalled that at some point in time Thanksgiving became more meaningful for his family. Almost at the same time, they realized that traditions had a beginning. Before there was a tradition, there was a single event. So they decided that in honoring the family tradition of being together on the holidays, they would host Thanksgiving dinner for both their families. Now, they could be the standard-bearers of the Thanksgiving tradition of the family community. The first year was a huge success, and both families readily agreed to return the next year. What Kali and Dudley learned and shared as guests on the television show, was the power of establishing family traditions.

While this couple's experience is about starting new traditions, vertical communities also pass along the perspectives of previous generations and can provide guidance regarding practices that have worked over generations. Old traditions and practices may foster respect, communication, enjoyment and even tolerance. Most vertical communities have stories from ancestors, some almost mythical, that demonstrate and reinforce the positive functioning of relationships. They tell us perhaps how our parents got along and how they dealt with such issues as financial stress. They also demonstrate what the future for a young couple might look like.

Exercise: Remembering Family Rituals and Traditions

This exercise is designed to have you remember or discover the rituals and traditions that are the pillars of your vertical community—what they are, when they started and how you learned about them.

THINK: Think about the most memorable traditions and rituals in your family when you were growing up. These might include holiday rituals, such as opening gifts in a particular way or at a particular time, or Mom always cooking the turkey and Dad always carving the bird, or non-holiday rituals, such as going out to dinner to celebrate a child making the school honor role.

DO: Write a list of the ten traditions and rituals that each of you liked the most, who made them possible and at what age you first participated in them. Write down who taught you about these traditions and rituals (parents, brothers and sisters, relatives) and if they are still being followed by your parents or in your own relationship with each other and your children.

You might want to call your relatives to share what you are doing, check out their recollections and find out which traditions and rituals they still follow.

SHARE: Compare your lists and discuss which traditions and rituals you still adhere to or would like to continue.

Horizontal communities

When seeking the support of a community, couples often look to their elders or families, but they also turn to *horizontal communities*, including peers and religious groups. Others around us, people we see every day, can provide us with information on how to be Couple and an opportunity to talk about what we are experiencing. These individuals are often experiencing or have experienced the same things that we are going through. Neighbors, friends from work, people we know from our church, synagogue or mosque, all of them can be supportive. They may show us what they have done that was successful—or, perhaps, not successful—and they may listen and provide coaching or advice when requested.

Patty and Frank were newcomers to their neighborhood in a small Southern city. They had moved for his job a year earlier and were struggling to feel comfortable. Their two small children were a handful, and Patty spent most of her time getting them to and from school and to their various after-school activities. Patty and Frank argued a great deal over having time for themselves and watching the kids. Patty was at home and in charge of the kids and their schedules all day and waited for some relief when Frank got home. Frank worked hard all day and wanted to relax and rest when he arrived home. He was also feeling pressure to spend more time at work and did not feel that Patty was on his side. Both of them felt tired all the time and unsupported by the other. Patty was considering taking the kids and going back to live with her parents in the Midwest. Frank had fleeting thoughts that maybe it would be better for them to separate for a while, until he got everything at work straightened out. They came to see Phyllis for therapy and to decide whether or not to separate.

Patty and Frank were feeling isolated and alone. They felt out of touch with each other. After one week in treatment, Phyllis gave them the assignment to meet some other couples. They argued with her that they barely had time for each other and the kids, let alone other people, but she persisted. That next week Patty met a neighbor up the street who had come to the door, looking for a lost dog. She invited the young woman and her husband over for a drink that weekend. Within three months, they were good friends, eating at each other's houses regularly and exchanging child-care duties. Through this couple, Patty and Frank met two other couples in the neighborhood, and the four couples had regular barbecues in the summer. Patty would often speak with the wives about concerns she had about her marriage, and they readily began sharing ideas about how to make their relationships better. Frank and Patty were now part of a horizontal community of couples that provided mutual support and nurturance.

Some horizontal communities of couples develop out of existing friendships. Close friends who form an informal couple community increasingly rely on social media to stay in touch. Social media, like Facebook and Twitter, are creating new opportunities for the expansion of such horizontal communities. Many of the couples in communities built on friendships contact each other on a daily basis. Darby and Lennie got married last summer. Four of their bridesmaids and six of their groomsmen had recently gotten married or were getting married within a year. It was sort of a traveling community of people who went from one wedding to the next, partying and celebrating. They all felt close to one another, and two couples decided to share an apartment for a year since finances were tight. Darby and Lennie talk and communicate electronically all the time with the other couples in their community. When they travel to other parts of the country, they often visit other couples in this community. Consequently, they really feel like they are part of a large, supportive network.

Whether couple communities are made up of friends, relatives in your own generation or neighbors, they provide day-to-day contact and support. If this is missing for you, it is possible to create it in a variety of ways.

Exercise: Hangin' with Our Friends

Who are the people of your own generation with whom you spend the most time? These are most likely the people who belong to your horizontal community of couples. You ask them for advice, watch how they behave and get support from them regularly.

THINK: Get together with your partner and think about the other couples you rely on the most when you need support, advice or help. Who assists you when you need a ride to the airport or runs an errand for you? When you relax on a long weekend or go to the beach, who is most likely to join you?

DO: Make a list together of the people in your horizontal community of couples. Speculate on whether these individuals would say *you* are in their community of couples, and place a check mark next to those you think would.

SHARE: Discuss the qualities of the people on your list. What do you most value about them? Are they loyal, friendly, generous, wise? Think about how they see you. What do you provide your horizontal community of couples? Are there some qualities or activities missing in your couple community? Discuss how you might want to expand your community.

Community Themes

You and your partner may benefit from horizontal communities that are organized around a specific theme, such as those listed below. While one particular interest may attract you to a community, the sense of connection developed there could allow for the shared pursuit of other activities. For instance, you may meet couples at a political gathering, then participate as a community in other activities as well.

Educational communities

You may want to explore becoming members of a learning or educational community. A shared learning experience or training not only serves a practical purpose, but it can be fun as well. Community college courses, cooking classes, sailing lessons or home-repair seminars serve to create a shared experience and also allow you to meet other couples involved in the same educational activity or training. Some educational activities may be specifically directed toward people in relationships, and those who take part in them may experience a sense of commonality or community. Marriage enrichment programs and couple communication programs fit into this category.

Brandi and Kevin had been married for ten years. A Romanticized Couple, they had lately been feeling that their life together was getting a bit boring. They were working hard at jobs they liked but did not love. They would come home, watch TV for a while and then go to bed. Their weekends were filled with chores around the house and visiting their aging parents in nearby assisted-living facilities. At the suggestion of a couple they met at a dinner party at Kevin's business, they decided to create a proclamation for their couple, one that would be exciting and romantic. They agreed upon "We dance together."

They loved their couple proclamation. It gave them energy, but it also gave them an idea. They enrolled in ballroom dancing lessons. Once during the workweek and at least once every weekend they took lessons and went out dancing. They met other couples in their class and went out with them, at first in town and then on weekend excursions to other nearby towns. They became committed to the lessons, but also to the dancing itself. They wanted to learn more dances. After a year, they converted their basement into a small dance hall. They would invite their friends to dance, and after a while they began to teach their friends new dances they had learned. They had created not only a community of couples but a group of new friends.

Sometimes the educational experience may be absolutely necessary for your couple. We found out Phyllis was pregnant on Mother's Day in the second year of our marriage. In those days, childbirth classes were still rather rare. Having our first child was a very exciting but scary prospect for us. We were living thousands of miles away from our parents and didn't have a lot of friends with young children. We joined a childbirth class and went to a session every week with seven other couples for twelve weeks. We all laughed together, got frightened together and listened carefully to our instructor. For many years we stayed in communication with our teacher and one of the other couples, and we followed the exploits of the couple's twin sons. These friends of over thirty years frequently remind us, "That group got us all through a lot."

Spiritual communities

Spiritual communities may be religious groups or communities where secular spirituality is valued. Couples may gather together to pursue such things as Bible study, meditation, celebrations of the solstice, consciousness-raising, tai chi or yoga, to name a few. What these communities have in common is the belief in some greater power or universal phenomenon. The idea that we are there to learn about some force or spirit that transcends our individuality often contributes to the power we experience as couples. For some spiritual and religious groups, marriage is considered sacred. They often focus on contributions people make to their *relationship* rather than to each other. It is the commitment to the marriage, to the couple, that is the godly act, not the commitment to the particular person. That notion is very consistent with our idea of commitment to the entity of Couple, rather than to a perfect partner.

Donnie and Corbin have been married almost fifty years and have been through a lot together. They have four children, nine grandchildren and two great-grandchildren. They are vital, active and very energetic. This was not always the case, however. About twenty years ago, with grown children living at home, one daughter getting divorced and Donnie losing her job as an accountant for a family-run business, they felt tired, unsupported, grouchy and in need of a break from the stress and from each other. Things came to a head when one day, while rushing to rescue their dog from a menacing young grandchild, Donnie slipped on a wet floor and took a bad fall. She was laid up for nearly two weeks, recovering from strained muscles in her back. She said that everyone tried to be nice to her, but most of the time she just wanted to scream in pain or frustration. Corbin was at a loss as to what to do. He was stressed, too, from managing the house as best he could, taking Donnie to physical therapy appointments and trying to keep her cheered up. He had thoughts some days of just leaving and not coming back.

One day Donnie's physical therapist recommended that she attend a tai chi class. He explained that tai chi was a martial art that involved slow and graceful methodical movements in a dance-like sequence. Donnie said she didn't want to do any more exercise, but her PT assured her, "Tai chi is more like meditation than exercise." Donnie attended a class and was blown away by how relaxing, fun and compelling it was. She immediately asked Corbin to come to tai chi classes with her. He did it for their couple and really liked it. Corbin and Donnie have studied tai chi together for nearly twenty years now, forming a close bond with their tai chi instructors. They taught their children the discipline and frequently lead family tai chi sessions during the holidays or when they all vacation together in the summer. The grace and harmony they now exude as tai chi instructors and as Couple is apparent to everyone who knows them.

Pursuing a spiritual or religious practice in groups, as a community, is a very powerful experience. It creates a feeling of belonging and enables you to experience your relationship as sacred or special.

Social communities

There are no real "couples bars," the equivalent of singles bars, for meeting other couples. However, social clubs organized around activities of interest to couples are essentially couple communities, places to meet other couples. Bridge clubs, co-recreational athletics, such as soccer, kick ball or softball, and, increasingly, online gaming provide opportunities to organize as couples. Doreen and Jimbo, a Romanticized Couple, had been married eleven months, after dating for nearly two years. He taught high school, and she worked for a software company. Doreen met Jimbo online, and she immediately wanted to find out if they shared an interest in a particular online game. Some of their first dates involved going online together as a team to play this game. Soon they recruited their couple friends to join them. One night a week and one day during most weekends the couples would gather together to play this game. They would order pizza and play for hours. After a while, they invited another couple to join them. These games turned into community events for Jimbo and Doreen, and they looked forward to them.

They also were in contact online with other couple players and began to chat online about each couple's style of cooperating and strategizing during the game. With the support of their gaming community, Jimbo and Doreen began to see that the strengths they had as a team while playing online could serve them in their daily life. They found out that Jimbo was a good "scout" in the game, and Doreen did thorough "battlefield cleanup." They focused on these strengths when devising fun strategies for tackling the grocery shopping and other chores.

What makes run-of-the-mill social activities or gatherings into community pursuits is the willingness to share what you have experienced and to get together regularly. Increased communication between members and shared experiences foster feelings of warmth, togetherness and reliability.

Exercise: Exploring and Creating Communities

THINK: As a couple, think about the activities you both enjoy and the interests you share. Make a list of the communities you are already a part of as a couple and those you would like to join.

DO: Look into how to join the communities on your list or participate in some of their activities. Take part in some of these activities together.

SHARE: Share your experiences after participating in these activities. Which ones did you like best? When would you like to do these activities again? Think about inviting other couples you know to join you.

Couples Coaching Couples

One of the most powerful communities we know for couples is one we co-founded twenty years ago. It is a community called Couples

Coaching Couples (CCC). It was a local community in the beginning but is now established around the country, with hundreds of couples participating in it. Couples Coaching Couples (www.couplescoachingcouples.com) is an organization committed to helping couples have profoundly fulfilling relationships. As mentioned earlier, we have found that this is most readily achieved with the help of a supportive community, that is, a safe and inclusive group of people that serve as a support and a resource for each other. The mission of Couples Coaching Couples is to create an ever-growing community of couples who see the value in enriching the lives of other couples. The organization has been successful in helping its members cast aside habits that no longer serve their relationship, while uncovering and embracing new and exciting ways of connecting to their partners.

Couples Coaching Couples is dedicated to making couples' lives profoundly fulfilling, joyful and fun. Over the past twenty years, the organization has developed practices and methods to support couples, and these include coaching each other and meeting and sharing as a community of couples. Groups of couples, or "circles," meet regularly to talk about their relationships and support each other in designing and maintaining the kinds of relationships they have always wanted to have. Pairs of couples from these CCC circles meet or talk weekly to coach each other on creating a powerful and dedicated relationship. Through a structured process of coaching, couples alternate listening to the other couple and then being coached on issues of their own choosing, which are often related to intimacy, communication, productivity, love and the full enjoyment of each other. Through the coaching process, partners learn to function together not just as cooperating individuals but also as a unified entity with its own goals and aspirations.

Couples Coaching Couples is a not-for-profit corporation which selects representatives of its member circles and holds national meetings and conventions. The only requirement to become part of this community is to acknowledge that you are a committed couple willing to both coach another couple and be coached by them.

Couples Coaching Couples communities and circles

Couples Coaching Couples was not designed as a therapy program in any way. It is merely a community of couples that practice actively supporting one another as couples through a defined method of coaching. Everyone coaches and everyone gets coached every week. The process of coaching begins when a committed couple joins a "coaching circle." After declaring their interest or meeting with a couple already in CCC, the couple answers some questions about their commitment to each other and then attends a circle meeting. Circles are composed of anywhere from four to sixteen couples. These circles meet every three months. At these "quarterly meetings," couples share what they accomplished over the last three months, how things are going, and what they learned from coaching another couple and being coached. One of the most interesting facets of the CCC community is that people are coached as a couple and by a couple. Each member of the "quartet" learns how to accept coaching and how to be an effective coach. At each quarterly meeting all the couples present put their name in a hat and draw the name of the couple they will coach and be coached by for the next three months. In this way, couples in the community get to know each other better and learn that good coaching is not just about a particular set of coaches, but is a process of listening and practicing.

How Couples Coaching Couples works

Once a couple enters the CCC community, they work with their coaching couple in a similar way every coaching quarter. At the start of a quarter, couples, with the help of their coaches, create a *declaration* for the couple that the two partners will use during the next three months. The declaration, like the couple proclamations we describe in Chapter Three, is a vision statement for the couple's relationship. It is an expression of who the partners are for each other for the foreseeable future. This "creation" phase is supported and monitored by the coaching couple.

On a weekly basis thereafter, usually on the phone, the quartet is in communication. They start by declaring themselves as a quartet committed to the process of CCC. Then the first couple states their declaration and reports how they have been operating as Couple in terms of their declaration. The other couple coaches them, examining what is happening in their relationship within the context of their declaration and suggesting homework for them to do the following week. Homework might be a request that the partners take time every day to say their declaration, or take time out for "tea for two" or a discussion about what they are feeling or doing, or it might be a larger project the partners take on as part of learning to cooperate on fulfilling the vision for their relationship that they created with their declaration. After twenty to thirty minutes of coaching, the couples switch roles and those who were being coached become the coaches.

At the end of a quarter, all the members of a local circle meet to report their experiences, share the completion sheets they filled out that summarize their accomplishments over the last twelve weeks, review some of the principles from the CCC Manual and get training from peer coaches. At the circle meeting, members often enjoy social time and a meal or snack together and plan other group activities over the next three months.

Brenda and Jack began Couples Coaching Couples a few years after the birth of their daughter April. They were a very happy and productive couple in many ways, deeply religious, civic-minded and active. Still, there were areas of stress for them as they began to take on projects, like supporting two small businesses and renovating an old farmhouse. Their CCC declarations helped them focus on the tasks at hand as well as the resources each of them brought to their relationship. With coaching from their quartet couple, Roberta and Will, they created the declaration "We are partners." It brought them to life every time they said it. It created a way of working cooperatively together, which they had not experienced before. During that quarter, they made significant progress on the farm and in their businesses.

They also noticed that April, their daughter, took a real interest in what they were doing. At age five, she was curious about what they were saying when they recited their declaration. They told her, and she asked to join in every day when they said their declaration. Perhaps she sensed the powerful feelings between her parents when they repeated it. In fact, over the next months, whenever she felt that there was anger or tension between her parents, she would say, "You guys had better say your declaration." At their next CCC quarterly meeting, Brenda and Jack and Roberta and Will had a chance to talk about the experiences they had had coaching and being coached and the results they'd enjoyed during the quarter. Each couple coached with a different couple the next quarter and had a chance to invent new declarations.

Reports compiled from interviews and surveys of participants in CCC have been very positive. Although not all couples remain in Couples Coaching Couples long term, most circles have veteran couples who have reaped the benefits from this work for decades. Very few couples who have participated in CCC have divorced, and a number of unmarried participants have decided to acknowledge their commitments by getting married or having commitment ceremonies.

It seems clear to us that Couples Coaching Couples is so successful because it supports partners in all Four C's of Couple Power. First, it requires that a commitment to the relationship be present at the outset and that this commitment be formalized by the creation of a couple proclamation, such as "We are partners."

Secondly, couples in CCC take on projects or activities that require cooperation. If this skill is not present, there is regular coaching available to help the couple learn and practice it. There are also mechanisms for the couple to be held accountable for what they said they would do: the couple must fill out summary completion sheets and speak at CCC quarterly meetings, noting in both cases what they have accomplished and what they have learned.

Thirdly, CCC fosters communication. Coaching sessions held on a weekly basis support communication between the partners, and they also learn how to speak as Couple to another couple. Many of the homework assignments are geared toward developing communication skills and thus provide practice in speaking clearly, directly and with a sense of commitment to each other and listening without judging one another.

Finally, it is clear that CCC fosters community, because it *is* a community. The regular meetings, social events and coaching sessions, both by phone and face-to-face, are opportunities for community interaction and foster feelings of belonging. The CCC national convention, held once a year in the city of a sponsoring circle, affords members of the CCC community a view of just how large the community is and reminds them that all around the country people are working on forging fulfilling, joyful relationships.

Donna and Billy met shortly before they started Couples Coaching Couples. They were both in their fifties. Donna had been married three times before, and Billy, while never married, had two previous long-term relationships. While dating, they heard about CCC from a friend and decided they were committed enough to their couple to become members. They joined a CCC circle and immediately noticed that the people around them were committed to their success as Couple. With the coaching they received, they learned to communicate up front their feelings, their concerns and the hopes they dared to have about their new relationship. Given the opportunity in Couples Coaching Couples to actually coach others in relationships, they began to build confidence in their own capacity to have a fulfilling relationship. Within a year of starting CCC, they got engaged, and a year later they married. The ceremony included their families, of course, but everyone in their CCC circle attended, too. The ceremony incorporated declarations, couple visions and many of the elements of CCC coaching. Family members and non-CCC friends commented on the amazing community feeling present at the wedding. They felt inspired by the ceremony and the spirit of those in attendance. Donna and Billy, who have been married now for seven years, are a truly happy couple. They have even assumed the leadership role of "Source Couple" in their CCC circle.

Couples Coaching Couples is just one organization that promotes community as an essential component of lifelong love. There are likely other couple community organizations around the country committed to supporting lifelong partnership.

Hopefully, the movement for couples community will continue to grow around the world, providing the crucial support that all couples need.

A Final Word about Community

Of the Four C's of Couple Power discussed in this book, community is the most exciting for us. It encompasses the possibility of a worldwide change in how relationships are supported. It is people helping other people and couples being committed to other couples that will ultimately break down the many barriers that keep people from committing, cooperating and communicating as couples. The power of friendship and mutuality reduces fear and increases our feelings of harmony, our sense of possibility and our humanity. We talk more about the possibility of this power, Couple Power, in Section III.

III

Challenges and Possibilities in Daily Life

CHAPTER SEVEN

Applying the Four C's:

Overcoming Outside Challenges to Lifelong Love

"Fortunately, we are born not simply with the tendency toward being self-centered but also with capacities for cooperation and sacrifice."

—Aaron T. Beck, *Love Is Never Enough*

As we have seen, once you get past the beginning romantic stage of your relationship, it is particularly important to be aware of the Four C's in order to maintain a strong couple and facilitate lifelong love. As the title of psychologist Aaron Beck's book declares, "love is never enough." Neither can we count on having children to keep us together. As wonderful as children are in their own right, they can create an even bigger challenge to Couple. While we need to attend to our children's needs, we must continually pay attention to the needs of our couple as well, so as to confront successfully the challenges of everyday life together. It doesn't sound so difficult, but most couples admit they have a problem nurturing their couple over time.

So given all the tools available for creating and maintaining a fulfilling relationship, we need to ask once again, "Why is it that lifelong love is the exception rather than the rule?" The rate of divorce in the United States has been over 50 percent for first marriages for quite a while now, with the rates for second and third marriages even higher. It does seem that it is not getting any easier to establish and maintain a fulfilling relationship today. Being part of a couple no longer means just caring for "hearth and home." The modern relationship is also expected to meet all the romantic and emotional needs of each partner. This often leads to utopian ideals and unrealistic expectations, which may stifle the relationship from the start. And those expectations are even greater now that our life expectancy is much longer. The reality is that committing to a relationship over time is not only rare but also extremely challenging. There are few models for accomplishing such a feat and many challenges and obstacles in the way. There are situations and conditions that we confront every day that make being in a relationship difficult. In addition, significant life events, like the birth of a child, an extramarital affair, a serious illness, an aging parent or a death in the family present huge challenges to a relationship and impact each partner in unique ways.

When life presents these situations and issues, it is important to take a step back and look at what you are reacting to in your environment and within yourself that may be blocking your commitment to creating and maintaining lifelong love. To begin with, you may be overlooking the significant effects that the broader culture has on you and your relationships. (By *culture* we mean the scope of behaviors and patterns communicated from one generation to the next through our language, biology and technology.) The broader culture, the environment in which you find yourself, as well as your own personal history may contribute to the difficulties of maintaining a fulfilling relationship. Being aware of these challenges helps you confront them together in powerful ways. Several examples of how we ourselves and couples we have known and worked with over the years have accomplished this are described in this chapter and the next. What we present here is by no means an exhaustive list of the challenges couples face, and many of the challenges overlap, but you are sure to see yourself in here somewhere.

Do not get discouraged when you confront these challenges. As we have seen in reviewing the tools available for achieving the Four C's, there are many productive ways to deal with them, and we may also use what we learn along the way to create new options for problem solving. With knowledge comes power—power to adapt and change. As you read about the numerous challenges described here, remember that whatever the difficulty, you have the tools of the Four C's to use as a couple and make a real difference in your circumstances.

Here is where the rubber meets the road, so to speak. It is not enough to simply understand or talk about your relationship problems. Talk is cheap. You must take action as a team and apply the tools you learned in the previous chapters. To maintain lifelong love, you must continually sharpen and use these tools. Anything worth doing takes practice, and that is nowhere more true than in keeping your relationship alive and well. All the challenges described here may be seen as opportunities for practicing the Four C's in your own life. So forge ahead and practice, practice, practice!

Individualism

Paula and Joel had been married for several years and had three young children. Paula quit her job to stay in their comfortable home in Georgia and raise the kids, while Joel worked to support the family. Her parents had moved to live near them and to help take care of the kids. Everything seemed just fine, until Joel's business started going downhill. One night he came home from work and excitedly announced to Paula, "I got a really good job offer today in Arizona! The job starts in two months, and they'll pay to move us. I told them right away that I'd take it. Isn't that great?" Instead of the joy and relief Joel expected, Paula was shocked and annoyed. "I knew you were looking for other jobs, but I didn't think you would decide to take one without talking to me first!" she exclaimed. She felt left out and cheated by his decision, and she did not want to disrupt her life to move. Joel felt defensive and betrayed by her reaction but went ahead and took the job, commuting to Georgia on weekends whenever he could. Paula was still upset and considered separation and even divorce. Eventually, after counseling with Phyllis, she decided to move with the kids to Arizona to be with him, but she said, "If he ever does this again, it's over!"

Paula and Joel, a Self-Focused Couple, were up against a culture of individualism, which provided them little preparation for the dilemma they faced as a couple. They were both stuck in their self-focused pattern and had no support or good models for how to be Couple. Paula's parents even encouraged her to come live with them when the going got rough. Paula was tied to her parents more than to her marriage, and Joel was operating as a "Lone Ranger." Both of them were thinking more about themselves than about their relationship.

Our individualistic culture, described in Chapter One, no doubt contributes to so many couples choosing to divorce rather than to stick it out and face their challenges together. In a throwaway society such as ours, if the relationship isn't meeting your needs, it may seem easier to get a new one than to work on correcting the situation. The recent increase in single-person households in the United States, both with and without children, is likely a sign of individuals choosing personal independence over couple attachments. The apparent strong desire for individuality and autonomy in American culture—what historian and social critic Christopher Lasch calls "the culture of narcissism"—contributes to the obstacles to lifelong love in modern society. Everywhere we look, the individual is the focus. In professional tennis, for example, the singles players, not the doubles players, receive the big money and the prime-time attention.

Now is the moment for couples to share the spotlight. What is needed for this to happen is support for a culture of connection that values both individualism and "couplism," honoring both the individual and the relationship. It is not that individuals should be unimportant; they are important. But we must avoid the extremes of narcissism and also support people in relationships. We need to acknowledge the important role of both individuals and couples in society.

Paula and Joel eventually realized how their individualistic attitudes were damaging their marriage, and they made a commitment to their couple. They started out with small steps. Their first proclamation was "We are building trust," and then they moved on to "We trust each other." They started acknowledging each other's contributions to the relationship every day. After Paula moved to Arizona, they created a new proclamation, "We are building a loving home together," and began celebrating their accomplishments, such as getting a renter for their house in Georgia and getting the kids settled in their new school. Things did not always go smoothly, but they learned to look together for new options. For example, when money got tight, Paula started looking for a job for the first time in five years. She realized that she was still angry about Joel's unilateral decision to move to

Arizona, so they did the "Clearing It Up" exercise, which appears in Chapter Five. This led to their scheduling several "tea for two" conversations, during which Paula asked to be acknowledged for being willing to relocate to Arizona. They both admitted that they took the people who were most important to them for granted. Their last step was to work on developing a new community of support to replace Paula's parents, upon whom they had become dependent. They began to reach out to other families in the neighborhood, started volunteering in local organizations and gradually began to feel a part of their new community. This also lead to an improved relationship with her parents.

Workplace and Career Issues

Sandy and Ken had been happily married for two years. They both had jobs they liked, Ken as a travel agent and Sandy as a teacher. Everything was fine until Ken was required by his agency to take on the job of traveling to various locations to assess the resorts there. He was not allowed to bring his wife with him, as it was thought that this would distract him from his work. At times, he would make these visits with other travel agents. After a few months of this, Sandy began to feel lonely and even suspicious of his interactions on these junkets with his female coworkers. Soon they began to argue and question each other's trust in their relationship.

The dilemma that Sandy and Ken experienced is a typical example of workplace pressures pushing partners apart. Even when both people are working at similar jobs or together, the workplace can take its toll on a relationship. Within our culture of individualism, the workplace emphasizes individual productivity:

produce and achieve as much as possible at all costs. The impact on relationships is often a sense of isolation and abandonment, and competition for time and attention. Sandy, for example, felt like she had to compete with Ken's coworkers for his interest and time. She came to fear that his loyalty to the company took priority over his marriage and that his attraction to the job superseded his attraction to her.

Sandy's concerns were well-founded. A recent national survey revealed that given human beings' limited bonding capacity, spending extended hours in the workplace lessens the degree to which we bond with members of our family and increases the likelihood of office romances. When individuals commit more time and energy to intimacy at work than at home, their intimate relationships suffer. Instead of an individualistic work ethic, we need a "couple ethic" that allows for career fulfillment without ignoring, stressing or devaluing the couple. Where a couple work ethic seems vitally important is in dual-career relationships. Both partners are busy and committed to work responsibilities. Some partners don't even work the same shifts or at the same time of day. Others must travel. Some couples carry on long-distance relationships in order for both partners to keep their job. Some companies make it difficult for couples and families to be together.

One of the first things Sandy and Ken did when they came in for counseling was to create the proclamation "We are a sharing couple." Then they started sharing and consulting with each other specifically about their jobs. When Ken was away on travel agency junkets, he would contact Sandy twice a day by phone, email, text or Skype and would consult with her about the places he was evaluating. At the same time, Sandy would talk about what was going on in her classroom that day and would get ideas and feedback from Ken. He told his boss about how helpful these consultations with his wife were, and eventually the company agreed to let Sandy go on some of the trips with him. Sandy also included Ken in her work by having him come to school with her one day and introducing him to her students and colleagues. No longer did they feel like they were on two completely separate tracks; they felt connected and supported even when they weren't physically together.

Finding ways to manage the household and child rearing on top of working outside the home is an added challenge for couples. Often the only way partners know how to do it is to alternate responsibilities. Bonnie and Brad were a dual-career couple, both in the real estate business, who had it down to a science. On a typical day, she would pick up their girls, Leila and Sara, after school, would drop Leila off at soccer and then would take Sara to ballet. She would wait there for Sara to finish and then would pick up something for dinner and go home. Brad would swing by soccer practice after work and get Leila and then would meet up with Bonnie at home. They would have a quick dinner together before Bonnie went off to choir practice. Brad would do homework with the girls and then would go to the gym to work out when Bonnie returned, and he would be back in time to help get the girls to bed. Then, if all went well, they would collapse into bed about 11:00 p.m., completely exhausted, with the alarm set for 6:30 a.m. On the weekends, there were soccer matches to go to, recitals to attend, shopping to do and chores around the house to tackle.

Bonnie and Brad loved each other, but since the girls came along, there seemed to be no time for just the two of them to be together. They were devoted to their children, but it seemed like parenting was a barrier to their relationship. They were too tired for lovemaking and too busy to slow down. The pressure on both of them at work to finish more projects and sell more real estate was hurting their marriage. It seemed like there were too many outside demands on them and not enough time or energy for passion and romance. To make matters worse, they were beginning to find coworkers, particularly those of the opposite sex, more interesting and available than each other.

As much as Bonnie and Brad loved them, their children had become a barrier to their satisfaction as a couple. They bought and read a number of self-help books and talked to their friends about the problems they felt comfortable sharing. But the books and their friends merely convinced them even more that things were going badly. Finally, they decided to seek counseling. Working with Phyllis, they came to see that they were each doing their own thing and that they were drifting apart. Bonnie and Brad created the proclamation "We are a powerful team" and began saying it every morning before they left for work and every evening when they returned home. They found that it really helped them feel more connected and that it improved their mood. Examining the commitment they had to the couple and their family as an entity, they began to invent ways of being together that could serve their couple. They took on dealing with their children's needs as a community, setting up carpooling and babysitting arrangements with neighbors, friends and family members. Brad asked for some time off from work, and Bonnie asked her parents to come and spend a few days with the kids so she and Brad could go away for the weekend.

Fortunately, more and more companies are realizing the stress on families due to workplace demands and now offer such things as on-site babysitting services and exercise programs, as well as flextime for managing dual careers and home life. In 1999 the American Psychological Association began identifying and honoring some of these businesses with its annual Psychologically Healthy Workplace Award. It is, indeed, gratifying to see the differences these companies are making in the lives of families and the benefits that are accruing to them from these progressive practices.

Money and Finances

Karen and Rick had been happily married for years, both of them with successful careers. They were doing so well that Rick decided to quit his job and start his own business, which he had wanted to do for years. They both agreed that this was a good idea. However, after several months of the business making very little money, they started to argue about how Rick was running the company and how he was spending his time. Karen thought that Rick wasn't working hard enough at it and that he was spending too much money. They were struggling financially, and it was taking a toll on their relationship. Rick felt constantly criticized, and Karen felt angry and betrayed that he wasn't doing his share to keep them solvent. They stopped going out together in order to save money, and they began to have little interest in having sex.

Such financial woes are all too common these days. The 2009 "State of Our Unions" report by the National Marriage Project indicates what many couples already know—that many of them were hit hard by the 2008 recession. Given the continued economic turmoil, financial challenges—unemployment, mounting credit card debt, even bankruptcy and foreclosure—have affected couples in record numbers. What makes matters worse is that partners often blame each other for their financial straits, rather than the economic forces in society, and take out their frustrations on each other. All these negative emotions build up, leading many times to severe emotional and physical distress. All too often individuals deal with this distress by drinking, smoking or eating too much.

Even though couples often rank finances as their number one stressor, that doesn't mean they necessarily discuss their financial affairs. On the contrary, couples tend to avoid the topic of finances, even more than talking about sex. Newlyweds Ralph and Anne, a Romanticized Couple, are a perfect example of a couple that practices this kind of avoidance. Anne had a lot of debt to pay off when they got married. She was embarrassed about it and rarely talked about it with Ralph, expecting him to be critical or angry. Instead, she took on a second job to prove to him and herself that she could contribute responsibly to their financial well-being. But instead of helping their relationship, her extra work ended up creating more stress for both of them. Like Karen and Rick, they ended up having little energy left over for sex or intimacy, which only magnified the tensions in their marriage.

In couples counseling with Peter, Ralph and Anne came to realize that they could take on her debt together. Ralph was easily able to contribute more financially. Anne quit her second job and was able to do more of the things around the house that she wanted to do, which Ralph acknowledged her for frequently. They understood that Ralph wasn't "rescuing" Anne, and that they were both contributing to the health of their couple. They paid off the debt in a short period of time and had much more energy to enjoy their life together.

It's well known that economic distress leads to higher levels of family tension and instability. This is true whether a household has too little money or even a lot of money, because people react to their imagined economic circumstances rather than their actual income. Arguments often ensue about how to spend money, especially if one partner is making more money than the other. However, while we might expect economic pressures to lead to an increase in divorce, the opposite is actually the case. Statistics show, for instance, that the divorce rate actually fell in 2008, when the country was mired in a recession. This may be partly due to some couples wanting to postpone divorce until their financial situation had improved. Looking at the prospect of having their income cut in half, many people may wait until they can better afford to get divorced. History shows that after times of war, there is often a baby boom. In a July 13, 2009 editorial, *Los Angeles Times* columnist Gregory Rodriguez suggested that we prepare ourselves for a "boom of an entirely different sort," namely a divorce boom. Other commentators have echoed this sentiment. It will be interesting to see if after the current economic malaise subsides, there is, in fact, a spike in divorce.

At the same time, a recent Pew Research Center study found that many couples believe that their financial challenges actually bring them closer together. Any challenge, including a financial one, can be surmounted if you take it on as a team. External challenges provide an opportunity for increased cooperation between partners. That was the case for Karen and Rick as they tackled the issue of Rick's flagging business as Couple. They did the "Clearing It Up" exercise, which helped them to get past the blame and guilt and start cooperating on managing the business together. They decided to hire an employee, and soon the business started growing. They had more time to spend with each other and even went to a couples' intimacy weekend workshop, which invigorated their sexual experience. Getting through this financial crisis gave them a new appreciation for their relationship in all areas of their life.

Not all couples want to combine their financial assets when they marry; however, Phil and Paula, the Dynamic Couple mentioned earlier, chose to keep their assets separate when they got married, which created some interesting challenges when Phil moved into Paula's house. At first, Phil found himself deferring to Paula about house matters, because it was "her house," and that left Paula wondering if he was really making it his home. Then they started doing remodeling projects together, with both of them putting their thought, labor and money into the house. The ownership of the property continued to be a significant factor in their financial planning, but after a while, they reported that "the combination of Phil's financial investment, our shared tasks and our joint decisions about major remodeling projects created what was so important to both of us, the experience that this is 'our home.'"

A similar issue faced Helen and Michael, the Self-Focused Couple mentioned in Chapter Five. Helen and Michael had kept their finances legally separate from the time they got married. This arrangement fit each of their cultural beliefs, as Helen said that in the Asian country where she came from women are in charge of the money. Michael maintained that in the United States, it was the man who was in charge. So they decided to split their assets and incomes. It wasn't until they were in therapy that they noticed how this arrangement had contributed to their becoming increasingly distant from each other. They got anxious even talking about money, let alone sharing it. They had no couple model for dealing with money. Then they created the proclamation "We talk and listen with all our hearts and all our might." Soon they felt more comfortable talking about money and made an appointment to meet together with a financial manager to explore legally merging their finances for retirement. After those meetings, they began to feel more trusting and open in the area of finances, as well as in other aspects of their life, such as their sexual relationship, discussed later in this chapter.

Gender

Ted and Jill, a Traditional Couple, were happily married, had two children, ages six and eight, and were eagerly awaiting the birth of their third child. Ted had a good job with a computer company, and Jill was just finishing her nursing degree. Jill wanted to hire someone to watch the baby a few months after the birth so that she could continue with her classes. Ted thought that no one but the parents should stay with the baby. He was confused as to why she did not feel content performing her "most important role as wife and mother." That was what his mother did. Jill saw things quite differently. While she expected it to be a challenge, she thought she could be both "a fully functioning mother and a career woman as well." She felt frustrated and angry that Ted would not support her desires, and Ted did not feel supported or acknowledged, either. "I'm doing my best to plan and provide for our family," Ted said. They grew increasingly stressed out and distant from each other.

It was not that Ted and Jill did not love each other or were not committed to one another. They were caught up in their expectations of what their gender roles should be, and it was the inflexibility of their attitudes about gender roles that was the challenge to their marriage. Their limited view of their respective roles and their inability to see those roles differently produced the problems, not the situation itself.

Many couples at this point say they have a "communication problem," when, in fact, the source of the problem is a failure to comprehend the fact that powerful cultural beliefs and traditions have locked them into a rigid pattern of behavior. The broader culture creates many expectations about gender roles. Once these expectations are internalized, they become strongly held beliefs that operate consciously or unconsciously in our relationships: "A woman's place is in the home"; "the man is the breadwinner and the head of the household." Even in the twenty-first century, gender stereotypes like these, unconscious or hidden as they may be, conspire against our adaptation to the inevitable changing circumstances of life. It does not have to be that way. But if gender roles are an issue for you and your partner, and you do not reevaluate and renegotiate your gender roles continuously, you risk having a rigid relationship or even one that fails altogether. How you think you should be deprives you of the opportunity to create how you *can* be. If gender expectations are creating conflict in your relationship, try the following exercise.

Exercise: Trading Places

THINK:	What things do you do each day in your relationship that are traditionally identified with your gender? Consider such home-related tasks as housework, errands and child care, as well as the arenas of your social life and household decision making.
DO:	Write down some of the home-related tasks you perform that are typical for your gender. Pick a day this week or next week to change places and perform the tasks that your partner has listed. (Note: A variation of this exercise is to take turns doing the other person's tasks together, as a couple.)

SHARE: Talk about what you have learned. Did it feel like you were at a disadvantage because of your gender? Would it be possible to share certain tasks or to divide responsibilities differently should the need or desire arise?

Husbands like Ted, who say it is inappropriate for their wives to do this or that, or that it is unmanly to do "women's work," such as changing diapers, limit their interactions with both their wives and children. When Ted was confronted in marital therapy with Phyllis about his use of the word *inappropriate* to describe Jill's desire to continue working on her nursing degree after the birth of their baby, he realized that his own point of view about child rearing came from his upbringing, and he was open to new ways of thinking about it. Phyllis then suggested that they do the "Trading Places" exercise for a few days. At their next session, Ted said that after trading places with Jill, he had a greater appreciation for all the time and work that Jill put into household chores, such as getting dinner on the table and the kids to their activities. He agreed to help out more around the house and support Jill in her educational pursuits. Jill acknowledged Ted for how hard he worked to keep them financially stable.

While their overarching roles did not change much, Ted did revise his gender expectations of Jill, giving her space to grow professionally. They approached the issues of child care and Jill's education and job search as Couple. Soon they found a babysitter that they both trusted, and Jill got her nursing degree and a part-time job that she loved. They still had to deal with the new challenges of being a dual-career couple, but since Ted had abandoned his rigid role expectations, they now were much more flexible and adept at finding solutions.

Women can be just as caught up in gender stereotypes as men. The wife who thinks she shouldn't be too "aggressive" may be reluctant to defend herself or to initiate certain actions. Nowhere is this reluctance more apparent than in the bedroom. The more passive role that women commonly assume in sexual relations with their partners may be a result of what has come to be called the "double standard," which, while much less prevalent among the younger generations today, still exists in many relationships. It dictates one set of "rules" for men and another for women, with men given more permission to be assertive and sexually active than women. When couples buy into such expectations, there is little room for growth or creativity in their sexual life. If the male partner is always supposed to be the initiator sexually, both partners may experience boredom, resentment, anxiety or disappointment.

Michael and Helen, the Self-Focused Couple described in Chapter Five and earlier in this chapter, had a mutually satisfying sexual relationship while they were dating. However, after several years of married life, Helen, who had grown up in a very traditional and restrictive home, became less interested in sex and rarely initiated it. After several years of this, Michael became resentful and resigned to his fate. They both felt sad and confused and eventually consulted Phyllis for sex therapy. Being able to talk about their feelings helped Helen let go of the restrictions of her past (she even got rid of her old traditional clothes), come to terms with the rape she suffered when she was eighteen and Michael's affair earlier in their marriage, and become "more clear about who I am." Michael became more gentle and sympathetic, a significant role change for him, and they both began enjoying sex and their relationship more. As they ended therapy, Helen said her favorite couple proclamation was "We are joyfully blissed out!"

When the feminist movement began in the 1960s, it confronted gender stereotyping and counteracted its debilitating influence to some extent, but it also increased pressure on women to meet often unrealistic expectations, imposed by others and themselves. For example, women may feel sexually inadequate if they do not engage in a variety of sexual experiences or have regular orgasms, which often leads to performance anxiety in the bedroom for both partners. In terms of careers, single mothers and women of lower socioeconomic status frequently have no choice but to work while they are raising their children. However, some women who do not need to work for financial reasons feel that it is not enough to fulfill the roles of wife and mother; they believe that they should have successful careers as well. On the flip side, working women nowadays face increasing pressure to be "perfect mothers," loosely defined as mothers who do not go right back to work after childbirth, who breastfeed for a year, who reject disposable diapers and who adhere to a host of other strict mothering guidelines. For working moms, it seems like you can't win either way.

Many women in this situation, with or without children, suffer from "superwoman syndrome," attempting to perform perfectly in a variety of roles simultaneously. Sometimes it all works, but more often than not, especially for dual-career couples, it creates stress and conflicts for both partners as the wife tries to "do it all." Studies show that even in dual-career relationships where the woman works full-time, she still does 75 percent of the housework. Unless couples address this kind of gender inequity, the prevailing view that domestic work is women's work, the female partner will likely experience increasing anger, guilt and unhappiness.

This is what started happening to us when Phyllis tried to be a "superwoman," raising two teenagers, seeing clients, writing a book, providing services for professional and volunteer organizations, organizing our social life and keeping up the house. "I wanted to do everything well," Phyllis said, "but it just didn't seem possible. I became easily irritated, and I realized that I was taking it out on Peter sometimes. There really wasn't much more he could do to help, but I continued to complain, anyway. I was also frustrated about not taking the time to do things, like painting and singing, that I really wanted to do." Eventually, we turned to some of our friends to help us find a solution. It actually took an "intervention" at our home, organized by a friend and with several other couples in attendance, to get a handle on this problem. The circle of people confronted and supported Phyllis, encouraging her to look at what she really wanted to do. When she realized that she needed to cut back on her practice so that she would have time for other creative enterprises, Peter agreed, and we took it on as Couple. Without that intervention, this book, a longtime goal, might have gone by the wayside, along with several other creative projects.

Men and women tend to have different styles of behaving and relating, and being aware of basic gender differences is useful. Women are generally more sensitive to context and pick up incidental information, while men are more narrowly focused and less distractible. Women use more nonverbal channels of communication and are generally more emotive, both verbally and nonverbally, than men; in conflicts, they may talk more, while men tend to be quieter. Neither behavior pattern is "better" than the other, but recognizing the differences may help us capitalize on them for our individual and mutual benefit.

Gender differences and gender-role expectations constitute formidable challenges to couples working to create a unique, satisfying relationship adaptable to changing circumstances. It may seem like there are few role models to refer to when looking for innovative solutions to gender-related issues, because we hear more about the failures than the successes. However, there are many couples who do make it work, more or less, as the success stories mentioned above attest. We just need to learn about these couples and pay attention to what works for them. The examples given here are meant to inspire you, but you might also want to go out and find some role models on your own.

Exercise: Role Models

THINK: Think about some of the couples in your life, past or present, that you admire. What makes their relationships work? What are some of their creative solutions to the very problems you are confronting?

DO: Ask at least one couple you know to share with you some of their strategies for dealing with issues in their lives. Share with them the things that you are working on and some of the solutions you have created.

SHARE: Discuss with each other what you learned from this couple. Look at how you might apply some of this couple's solutions to your own life.

Parenting

Not all the challenges of life are negative. Some of them, in fact, are quite positive, like weddings and children. Having children is one of those experiences that we usually expect to be joyous, and it most often is. However, those expectations in themselves may prove to be an obstacle to Couple, making it more difficult to face the realities of having children. If you expect everything to be blissful, and if you want to have only the joy and to ignore the pressures, when reality hits, you may be totally unprepared for handling it.

Our mothers might have told us that the path to happiness is to make money, get married and have children. They were partly right, in that people of higher economic status report higher levels of happiness across the board, and married couples report higher levels of satisfaction than unmarried couples—but only *before* they have children and *after* their children leave home. Parenting actually presents some of the most difficult of all challenges, whether they are raising your own children or your stepchildren, as we describe later. We are certainly not making an argument for not having children or not raising families together. Our own two children are the lights of our life, though bringing them up was not without its difficulties, as we will explain.

The challenge of having children can begin even before a child is conceived. An increasing number of women today experience problems with infertility. The tendency for women to have children later in life, along with increasing stress and pollutants and poor eating habits, all may contribute to this trend. The incidence of dysfunctions in men is also increasing, perhaps for some of the same reasons. The stress on couples who are trying to get pregnant and have problems with infertility is enormous. The financial and physical burdens of infertility treatments, along with the emotional upheaval caused by failed procedures and miscarriages along the way, are sometimes enough to make couples give up trying to get pregnant—and, unfortunately, even throw in the towel on their marriage. We know of incidents where the husband has divorced his infertile wife and married a woman more likely to bear children. There is certainly a long tradition of that, going all the way back to the kings and shahs who divorced, banished and even imprisoned their wives who did not bear a child or, specifically, the son they were determined to have. Fortunately, there are more contemporary examples of couples who have made it work.

Dianna and Bill, a Dynamic Couple in Couples Coaching Couples, had been trying to conceive a child for several years. As time went on, they started getting depressed and losing the joy they had in their relationship. Then their CCC coaches helped them see that their desire to be parents, in Dianna and Bill's words, "demanded that we see the world as it can be, rather than how it is." They worked on the possibility of adoption, and at the respective ages of forty-four and fifty, Dianna and Bill adopted a son. He was thirty-six hours old when they picked him up at the hospital and became his parents. Over the years, they have found that "having a young person in our life keeps us young."

Interestingly enough, once couples apply to adopt a child, they sometimes get pregnant, perhaps an indication of the negative impact of stress, which is suddenly eliminated, on getting pregnant. The pregnancy itself, when it does happen, has its own challenges. The mother may feel unattractive and unappealing, feelings that may give rise to depression or a reluctance to have sexual relations. The father may feel rejected or left out of the close bond that is already developing between the mother and the child. Some men even turn to other women for sex during this time, having affairs, which obviously creates another set of challenges for the couple. The husband may also feel left out if the wife does not share what is going on with her physically and medically. If she does not want her partner with her during prenatal exams, sonograms, Lamaze training or even child delivery, a disconnection in the couple bond may result.

This is what happened to Bill and Judy before the birth of their first child, because Judy was too embarrassed to have Bill in the delivery room with her. She was uneasy about how she would look during childbirth, and she said that her mother never allowed her father to participate in her delivery. Bill very much wanted to be there with her, and it caused a great deal of conflict between them. They worked on it in a marital therapy session with Peter and got clear about trusting their couple. They created a couple proclamation, "We trust our couple," and Judy agreed to have Bill there with her during the delivery. His presence made the whole experience more joyful and memorable for both of them.

Once the child is delivered, then the real challenges start, and they don't let up for a number of years. Fortunately, whatever the challenge, it doesn't last forever. The children do grow up, and each stage of child development has its own particular interesting characteristics. We remember flying to Florida to visit grandparents when our kids were one and four years old. One was crying, and the other was throwing up. We thought, *It can't get any worse than this!* Then the people in the seats behind us said, "Just wait. This is the easy part." That was quite an eye-opener, and we remembered their words each time the going got rough. We even created the proclamation "This is the easy part." This proclamation helped give us some perspective and a sense of humor about it all, which got us through until the teenage years hit.

Adolescence is demanding for parents and teenagers alike. It is an extended period of time during which children separate from their parents and develop their own identity. Parents often are reluctant to let go of their "babies," and children are faced with hormonal changes, more complicated social interactions and increasing academic responsibilities. Parents may disagree about how much freedom to give their children and how much responsibility to take for their children's lives. This may generate arguments, which only increase conflict between the partners and with the children. It is important to keep in mind that overprotecting and coddling our adolescent children may contribute to the development of that sense of entitlement so rampant in our individualistic culture. Certainly, children need love and support all along the way, but if we go overboard, we risk creating overly demanding children and shortchanging our couple, as we give up time for nurturing our own relationship.

Darlene and John, a Self-Focused Couple, hit a crisis point in their relationship soon after their son left for college. Darlene cried for days after she dropped him off at school. She showed up twenty minutes late for their next couples therapy session because she was talking to their son on the phone. She admitted, "Talking to my son at college is more important than anything else I can imagine." John was encouraged to share his feelings, which he did, saying that he had been feeling neglected by Darlene for the past several months. Darlene shared that she had been confiding in their son lately out of frustration with John, who seemed unable to speak any kind words to her or express affection. The challenge for Darlene and John was to realign their bond, to make their couple a priority. Toward this end, they started focusing more on their couple and began to be open and authentic with each other about what they were feeling. John said that he felt better just knowing that he was heard. They scheduled regular "tea for two" conversations and date nights, and they created the proclamation "We are Couple, and we are kind." They repeated their proclamation at least twice a day to underscore their commitment to their relationship.

Many dual-career couples, like Bonnie and Brad, discussed earlier in this chapter, often express sadness and guilt about not having enough time for their children, but they often forget about the impact of not having time for their *couple*. In fact, their relationship often comes last, as they tend to take each other for granted in order to meet their children's needs. Financial constraints and restrictive child-rearing practices, such as not being willing to leave children with a babysitter, may add to the difficulties of spending quality time together as a couple. The solutions that Bonnie and Brad, and other couples mentioned here, devised for balancing the roles of parent and partner are crucial for maintaining a strong couple relationship and fostering lifelong love.

One of the areas of a relationship that is particularly susceptible to injury is insufficient time for sex. Given our busy lives, it's difficult enough to find time and energy for sex under the best of circumstances, but it is particularly difficult once kids come along. The sleepless nights we have when we must tend to infants leaves little energy for intimacy. Privacy and spontaneity may be an issue once the kids are old enough to barge into the bedroom. Even showing affection in front of kids is difficult for some couples. Add to all these obstacles the differences in sexual desire and attitudes between partners, and you frequently have the perfect storm, as in the following example.

Stan and Sara, a Self-Focused Couple with two young children, came into therapy under a great deal of stress. Stan had recently lost his job, and he and Sara were having constant disagreements about the frequency of their sexual encounters. Sara, in full-time practice as a veterinarian, wanted to sleep in as long as possible before starting her day at 6:00 a.m., whereas Stan liked having sex in the morning and frequently initiated it. He felt rejected anytime that Sara didn't want to have sex, even though they had sexual relations one or twice a week. Both of them felt anxious and discouraged.

Sara and Stan created a proclamation, "We are a happy and successful couple," and they designed and implemented a project they called the "Passion Project" to deal with their love life more effectively. Sara agreed to initiate sex once a week, while Stan looked for ways to make the mornings easier for her. Just agreeing to work on the project and to be more generous about each other's needs almost immediately made them feel more connected. They began planning ways to bring more romance into their lives, creating a "date night" at home and planning a romantic getaway together. Stan asked his mother to babysit the children, and they went together to shop for sexy lingerie for the trip. Sara felt less pressured and more supported, and Stan felt more hopeful.

Another challenging situation for families is when children and parents compete for one another's attention. When this happens, conflicts may arise for the couple. For instance, when one parent spends a lot of time with the children, perhaps taking part in extracurricular activities, such as coaching a sports team, the other parent may feel left out. The partner may be so involved in these activities that s/he may not even be aware that the relationship is suffering. In cases like this, it is important to make your feelings known to your partner so that s/he understands the situation and the two of you can work on dealing with it together. This happened to us when our kids were teenagers and were active in sports. Once we discussed the issue, we were able to work out ways to be more attentive to each other's needs when we were dealing with the busy lives of a whole family.

The issues of bonding and feeling left out are particularly acute in blended families. Nearly one-third of all American adults have remarried, and there is little support or information to guide them in confronting their unique problems. Tensions may develop when dealing with ex-spouses and children from previous marriages, even if those children do not live in the home. It is important to agree as a couple how much each of you will interact with exes and children, and to support each other when challenging situations arise.

Earl and Dana, a Traditional Couple who married after his first divorce, faced the challenge of dealing with Earl's four grown children, all of whom were against his remarrying. Earl and Dana were disappointed about his children's rejection of their relationship, and they turned to their CCC coaches for advice on dealing with it. During the coaching, they were told to listen to each other's feelings about the situation and make a plan for dealing with his family as Couple. With Dana's support, Earl was encouraged to get in touch with his ex-wife and each of his children individually. Shortly thereafter, Earl's youngest son came to stay with them for a few days. When his mother came to pick him up, Dana invited her in to rest and have some lunch. After that visit, Earl's ex-wife called Earl and the other children and told them what a nice time she had. Ever since then, Earl's relationships with his children have been closer, and Earl and Dana have enjoyed many visits with all the children and frequent family gatherings. It eventually became clear that the children's resistance to their father's remarriage had to do with its potentially negative impact on their mother. When Earl and Dana reached out to Earl's ex-wife and helped her feel more comfortable, everything seemed to fall into place.

Family and Friends

When dating, Peter asked Phyllis to move with him to the city where he had just received a good job offer. This was a difficult decision for Phyllis because she really loved California and had many good friends and some possible job offers there. "It didn't make it any easier to commit to our relationship," Phyllis said, "that my friends didn't want me to leave." Peter, however, was convincing and persistent. In the end, Phyllis found a good job in the same city and decided to move with Peter—no thanks to her friends, however.

What Phyllis experienced with her friends is not an unusual social phenomenon. The natural tendency among groups is to keep everyone together. If someone should want to leave, they are usually not encouraged to do so because departures could threaten the existence of the group as a whole. When a single person becomes part of a couple and splits off from his or her group of single friends, the rest of the group may actively or indirectly discourage the relationship in order to keep the friend in the group either for the sake of group survival or out of jealousy. This phenomenon is called "network interference." In some groups of singles, the new couple is accommodated, but the change is not always easy for either the group or the couple.

Parents and in-laws may also cause network interference to couples. Such was the case with Paula and Joel, whose relationship issues are explored earlier in this chapter. When Paula did not want to move out of state with her husband after he got a new job, her parents encouraged her to stay put, even if it meant ending the marriage. They would rather have had her and their grandchildren live near them than deal with keeping Paula's marriage together. Fortunately for Paula and Joel and their children, they sought counseling, which, as we noted earlier, gave them a more objective perspective. Paula was able to separate from her parents and move to be with her husband, even without her parents' support. This led her to feel more independent and more connected to Joel, an important transition she needed to make in the interest of their lifelong love.

Dealing with network interference from in-laws, parents and extended families is never easy, but it is particularly difficult in families where parental approval of the potential spouse is required. Many cultures still operate this way, discouraging or even forbidding marriages to individuals of a different background, religion or ethnicity.

When Ravi, born in India and living in the United States, announced his engagement to Carol, a native New Yorker and non-Indian, his parents—who expected him to take an Indian wife—opposed the marriage and threatened to disown him. The pressure that Ravi's parents exerted on their son was so great that he and Carol considered breaking their engagement, even though they were very much in love and had much in common. Fortunately, their coaches in Couples Coaching Couples helped them clarify their commitment to Couple and cooperate as a team in dealing with Ravi's parents. They were encouraged to acknowledge each other's efforts and to listen to each other's difficulties without blame or criticism. After they got married, they went to India to visit Ravi's parents, who, seeing the love between them, came around and gave the couple their blessing.

Even where parental approval of the marriage is not required, parents may prove to be quite a force to be reckoned with if they don't like their child's choice of a spouse. Their disapproval may stem from a variety of issues, including differences in religion, race, educational attainment and economic status. If you get married without working out these disagreements with your parents, they will continue into your marriage and give rise to numerous arguments about how to handle in-laws. This impasse may get even harder to negotiate as your parents grow older or if they fall ill, especially if they must move in with you, as in the situation described below.

Sharon and Ron, the dual-career couple with two young children mentioned in Chapter Three, had to deal with this when, after Ron's father died, both his mother and grandmother moved in with them. His mother tried to help out with the children and around the house, but she always seemed to side with Ron whenever there were disagreements in the home. This created a lot of tension between Ron and Sharon, which eventually brought them to see Phyllis. They created the proclamation "We back each other up 100 percent" and almost immediately started envisioning new and productive ways to care for their children and their extended family as a team. They made an effort to have Ron's mother be a part of "the team" and invited aunts and uncles to come over and help them out as well. They began acknowledging each other every day for their contributions and accomplishments, and they soon became much happier.

Occasionally we may deal with the stresses in our life by confiding in someone other than our partner. Certainly, it is fine to share our trials and tribulations with family and friends, but if we do not confide in our partner, s/he may feel excluded. The partner who is left out may feel jealous and a need to compete with the other relationship or relationships. This kind of network interference is particularly common with colleagues from the workplace. One woman we counseled would go out with her girlfriends for a drink after work two or three nights a week. She would discuss with them things that were troubling her about work and her intimate relationship. Her husband felt progressively more and more isolated from her. When your child is the confidant, to the exclusion of your partner, the status quo gets thrown out of whack, and once again, your couple suffers.

The Internet and the Media

These days people often turn to social media when seeking to escape life's pressures, confide in another and find comfort. With the accessibility of sexual content and contacts online, electronic media can easily become a distraction and even an addiction, as with the following couple. Doug and Arlene, a Traditional Couple who had been married for several years, came for therapy after Arlene discovered that Doug was visiting sexual sites on the internet after she went to bed each night. He was even chatting with a woman he met online. "I felt terrible about it," Doug said. "But it just seemed to escalate the more I got into it." Arlene threatened to leave him if he didn't stop. In therapy, they began by looking at how much they cared about each other and got clear about their commitment to the marriage and their willingness to work on the issue as a team, creating the proclamation "We are a loving team." They scheduled more time to be together, especially after work and on weekends. Eventually, they rekindled their interest in being with each other and started going to sleep at the same time at night. They didn't have many couple friends or social engagements in their life, so they started creating opportunities for a community of couples to come together. They sponsored a Fourth of July potluck at the pool in their neighborhood and met many couples with whom they began to socialize. Soon their life together was fulfilling. It was obvious to them that their "loving team" had helped Doug get free of what had become an addiction for him and an obstacle for their couple.

Modern couples generally get most of their information and education about being a couple from the media, not educational institutions, churches or their own families. When family life courses are provided in schools, they usually give cursory treatment to couple and sexual issues, focusing primarily on sexual abstinence and sexually contracted diseases. Rarely are the challenges to couples and strategies for handling them covered in the classroom. In this technological age, we are constantly exposed to idealized images of couples on television, on the radio, on internet sites and in movies, newspapers, magazines, books, music and advertisements. These unrealistic representations of couple relationships shape our expectations and attitudes about our own relationships. For instance, the frequent ads on television and on the internet for drugs treating erectile dysfunction present idealized individuals and do not take into account couples' relationships. And we should add that while these medications are helpful in certain cases, when prescribed by a physician, the constant bombardment of commercials may also increase the pressure men feel to perform, increasing anxiety and raising unrealistic expectations.

Most television dramas and sitcoms present situations that are either hopelessly tragic or idealistically romantic. Rarely do we get to see couples work through everyday conflicts in a realistic way. Talk show hosts generally have the most volatile and negative couples on their shows, and they either berate them or "cure" them in one episode. Even worse than that are the reality shows that deliberately put couples in tempting situations to see if they will cheat on their partner. The shows that supposedly bring couples together don't do much better, as they are based on the romanticized model of two individuals finding each other rather than creating a lasting relationship together.

Jane and Arthur, a Self-Focused Couple, both working professionals, had been married for several years and had a three-year-old daughter. In the past several years, they had sex less frequently and Arthur had taken to watching X-rated movies and porno films several times a week. He bought Jane lingerie that resembled what he saw in those films, and he wanted her to wear it and perform the acts he witnessed in the films. At first Jane agreed, to please Arthur, but after a while she refused, telling him, "This feels degrading." Arthur became increasingly frustrated, and Jane became more angry and confused. They decided to work on their relationship together in therapy. During weekly sessions with Phyllis, they renewed their commitment to their family, creating the proclamation "We are present to love." As a result, Jane felt safer and was able to share an incident of sexual abuse she experienced as a child. Arthur and Jane found out more about each other's earlier experiences with sex and learned to accept each other's differences. They found other ways to express affection and discovered new erotic things to do and watch that they both found mutually gratifying.

The Legal System

The same legal system that legitimizes our marital contracts also adds complexity, directly and indirectly. It is important to be aware of this complexity and how it may impact your couple. Even before a couple marries, they may seek legal counsel to work out financial arrangements in their relationship. In some cases, their financial concerns are addressed in a prenuptial agreement, but sometimes the specifics of a prenuptial agreement ruffle the feathers of one partner, or cause a rift in the relationship. So while useful in some cases, the prenuptial agreement may not necessarily go very far toward making the couple an entity. And it may just be preventing the partners from fully trusting each other and taking the risk of commitment.

The legal regulation of marriage is perhaps the most problematic when couples are dealing with issues of divorce. While necessary in many cases, this regulation often hinders any possibility of future reconciliation for the troubled couple. Some exceptions to this may be found in recent developments in mediation, collaborative law and covenant marriage practices. Even with these options, many lawyers say that divorcing couples usually still choose to have their respective lawyers negotiate the divorce. Perhaps that is testimony to couples' continued lack of confidence in their ability to cooperate.

Sonia and Tom, a Traditional Couple who had been married for ten years and had three children, were separated when Sonia came to Phyllis for therapy. Her lawyer had advised her to remove all her money from their joint account and cease sexual relations with Tom, so as to establish a boundary of legal separation. She did these things, which increased Tom's suspicion about her motives and made him angrier and further decreased opportunities for intimacy between them. They met with Phyllis as a couple for a few sessions and began to work as a team on their differences. They stopped communicating through their lawyers and began cooperating to find new solutions to their problems. Shortly after that, they moved back in together and continued working on their relationship in couples therapy.

While challenging for all couples, the legal system's handling of marriage is especially problematic for same-sex couples. Same-sex marriage is not recognized by the federal government—and thus same-sex couples are denied the federal benefits and rights of marriage—but it is recognized in some states. Although some states have legalized same-sex marriage or legally recognize civil unions, most states do not and, therefore, same-sex couples do not have the opportunity to enjoy the rights and benefits afforded by the institution of marriage. The consequences of this can be serious. Same-sex partners may be barred from hospital rooms or making treatment decisions. And if their partner dies, they may be denied access to the funeral home or even their own home. If they had a child or children with their partner, they may lose all custody rights. The lack of legal recognition of their relationship often makes it difficult for same-sex couples to define their commitment to each other or to the children they raise. However, with a strong commitment to their relationship, they may find workable approaches to dealing with these issues.

Betts and Bobbi, a lesbian Dynamic Couple, had been living happily together for seven years and decided they wanted to adopt a child. However, they ran into many difficulties, since their state did not legally recognize their relationship and actually restricted LGBT adoption. They became very depressed about not being able to create a family and even considered separating. In therapy, they created the proclamation "We are family" and began exploring in greater depth options for adoption. They reached out to other couples in a similar situation and found out about promising avenues for adoption.

Intercultural and Interfaith Issues

So many of the challenges that confront couples today result from our diverse ethnic, racial, cultural and religious backgrounds. While this diversity has given rise to many wonderful relationships, which are enriched by the unique experiences and perspectives that the partners bring, it is also often the source of conflict and distress, especially among extended families. It is important to learn how to handle such conflict, so that it does not escalate and drive the couple to give up on their relationship, which frequently happens with such couples. Learning to appreciate each other's traditions is a place to start.

David and Luanne, a recently married young couple, were able to do that when planning their marriage and wedding. David was Jewish and Luanne was Catholic. They worked together by advocating for their marriage to their respective families, justifying the inclusion of both religious traditions in their relationship and in their wedding ceremony. From the beginning of their engagement, Luanne sent cards signed by both of them to David's parents on Jewish holidays, something even he had never done before. David spent Christmas with Luanne's family, decorating the tree and exchanging presents. Their wedding, presided over by a Jewish judge, began with the playing of "Ave Maria" and ended with the traditional Jewish breaking of a wineglass. Thanks to their commitment and openness, both of their families were able to adjust, thoroughly enjoying the wedding and lovingly supporting their marriage.

Interracial marriages are now commonplace, but the variety of challenges that interracial couples have faced historically, from ongoing societal prejudice to unaccepting families, seem no less prevalent. Both partners often adhere to a "code of silence" when it comes to their family histories. Whether it is a result of loyalty to family or just fear, this code of silence stifles communication and intimacy in the relationship and limits the support the partners could get from their extended families.

Julie and Mel, a young, interracial Self-Focused Couple who had been married for six months, came for therapy when they found out that Julie was pregnant. Mel's parents had been against the marriage from the start. They thought that an interracial marriage would be difficult for both of them to negotiate, and they feared that he would become alienated from his family community. Mel wasn't very close to his parents and didn't like to talk about them. Julie wanted their children to know their grandparents, and they began arguing about how to handle this. In therapy with Peter, they took on the issue as a team. Mel called his mother and told her that he and Julie both wanted them all to have a better relationship. Shortly thereafter, Julie contacted her mother-in-law by phone. She shared how much she loved Mel and how much he loved his mother; then Julie went to visit her mother-in-law for the weekend. When she returned, she told Mel what a great time she had. This helped Julie and Mel feel more supported and brought the whole family closer together.

War and Deployment

One of the most difficult challenges that anyone has to face is participation in a war or other military conflict. When one or both members of a couple are in the armed services and are deployed to the battlefield, it affects the whole family. When a partner is away from the family for a long period of time for any reason, it is stressful, but it is especially hard when your loved one is in the military and faces constant danger. The partner and children at home must deal with anxiety about the deployed loved one's welfare; the deployed partner must deal with both the stresses of combat and the emotional strain that accompanies a prolonged absence from the family. When the deployed partner comes home from war, the couple must face the psychological and sometimes physical trauma resulting from combat. Post-traumatic stress disorder (PTSD) is all too common in returning veterans. Even with professional help, couples may be unable to cope with the adverse effects of PTSD, and serious marital discord can occur.

What we have found to be most helpful for couples dealing with combat-related anxiety and trauma is learning how to confront their issues together. If you are about to be deployed to a combat zone, sit down with your partner as often as possible beforehand and talk about your feelings in a "tea for two" conversation, even if it is for just a few minutes at a time. Be sure to do some planning to manage the tasks that will have to be handled by the partner who will remain at home in the deployed person's absence. Together, you might also want to set up a blog or website devoted to your family, which the partner at home can add to as time goes on, so that the deployed partner can check in whenever possible and stay in the loop. You both might want to keep a journal or scrapbook of events to share with each other at the homecoming. In addition, you may wish to seek out some professional help ahead of the departure to learn ways to deal with the extreme stress of military deployment.

It was the second marriage for both Marilyn and Chuck, who was an Iraq combat veteran. Chuck had gotten divorced shortly after his return from Iraq and rarely talked about either his previous marriage or the war. He had been depressed for several months before he met Marilyn at a swing dance class. They both loved to dance and hit it off right away. They married a year later and were enjoying their life together until Chuck started getting depressed again. No longer did they go out dancing, and they stopped having sex due to a sexual dysfunction Chuck was experiencing. They went to see Phyllis for therapy, but Chuck still refused to talk about his time in Iraq, until they joined our couples therapy group. Only then did he feel connected and safe enough to start sharing about his wartime experience. At one group session, they reported that Chuck had started opening up to Marilyn that week about his feelings, and they had started dancing in their living room. They created the proclamation "We dance through life." Then Chuck shared some of the experiences he had in Iraq with the group and thanked everyone for their support. There wasn't a dry eye in the house.

Loss of a Family Member

During the course of our lifetimes, we face many losses that impact our couple in a variety of ways. *Miriam-Webster's Collegiate Dictionary,* 11th Edition, defines *loss* as "the act of losing possession." In our culture, we tend to get very attached to our "possessions," and it may require a good deal of adjusting to handle a loss and "let go." The loss of a family member is the ultimate loss. Couples that are flexible and are able to work together to adjust to change are best able to cope with the shock and trauma of losing someone in their family. Without that flexibility, one or both partners may blame the other for causing or doing nothing to prevent the loss. Even if the death occurred before you got together as a couple, it may still be traumatic for one of you and thus may impact the relationship. This is especially true in the case of the loss of a parent or a child.

Loss of a parent

Separation from our parents is something we all need to go through in our lifetime. In the natural course of events, our parents die before us, and we have to deal with their passing, as individuals and as a couple. The loss of our parents, especially if the feelings of grief are unresolved, may weigh heavily on us, affecting our partners as well. While grieving is a private experience, working on the feelings together as Couple may be very helpful to both partners. We saw this with Scott and Marilyn in Chapter Five. With couples therapy, Marilyn was able to acknowledge her grief for the loss of her father, who died when she was a little girl. She had been saying, "I didn't have a father," rather than accepting his death. Then she took Phyllis's suggestion to write a letter acknowledging her father and saying goodbye to him; once she did so, she could say "hello" to Scott. She stopped unconsciously trying to make Scott into her father, which could never work, and let him be a husband who loved her as a wife. It was so inspiring that Scott even wrote a letter to his own father, who had died when he was a teenager. He remembered what his father had said to him one night after he had to bail him out of jail, "You'll never amount to anything." In writing the letter, Scott was finally able to forgive his father and himself. Talking and grieving together about the loss of their fathers was a turning point for both Scott and Marilyn and brought them closer together.

A similar thing happened for Sara and Stan, who are mentioned in Chapter Five. They realized in the course of a therapy session that Stan still had a lot of anger toward his father, who had died a few years ago. Stan had never felt acknowledged or appreciated by him, and that was still affecting his self-esteem, which was a concern to both him and Sara. He agreed to write a letter to his father as a way to deal with these unresolved feelings. In their next therapy session, he read the letter aloud, including the part where he asked his father to some day give him a sign of his approval. Sara cried when she heard that and said, "You could give yourself permission to feel his approval right now. You deserve it!" That was a real eye-opener for Stan, and he agreed to do that. Sara said, "Now I can again see the man I married." By dealing with the loss of Stan's father and Stan's unresolved anger, Sara and Stan began to regain their couple.

Loss of a child

As difficult as it is to lose a parent, it can be even more challenging for a couple when a child dies. It is so devastating that many relationships do not survive the loss and end up in divorce. Parents can suffer this loss even before a child is born—during pregnancy, when there is a miscarriage. Miscarriages are common occurrences, and most of us do get past them, but it can be very difficult in the moment, and especially until there is another pregnancy or a child is born. Losing a child in infancy is especially painful and upsetting. The parents' feelings of guilt and anger may be overwhelming. Often the cause of death in infants is undetermined and is ruled sudden infant death syndrome (SIDS). While the incidence of SIDS has dropped since parents were first alerted not to put their infants to sleep on their stomach, thousands of infants still die of SIDS in the United States every year. Not knowing the cause of an infant's death makes it even more difficult to come to terms with it.

That was definitely the case for Aaron and Jeannine. When they came for therapy, Aaron and Jeannine were considering separation. They were devoted to their two-and-a-half-year-old son, but they were both still grieving the loss of their second child, who died from SIDS last year, at the age of six months. They both had little desire for sexual interaction. Aaron said that he felt disillusioned and "angry at God" and was afraid of "having the rug pulled out from under me." Jeannine felt shame for what she perceived was her failure to prevent their child's death. They had few friends and were fairly isolated. The best they could do at the onset of therapy was to create the proclamations "We are married" and "We are working together." Shortly thereafter, they joined Phyllis and Peter's couples therapy group, where they felt supported and connected to other couples. They followed through with the homework to have "tea for two" several times a week and began to feel great at surviving what happened. That was when they created the proclamation "We are grapes." It helped them, they said, to feel grateful and see the humor in life. They planted a tree in memory of their lost child, and by the time they left the group, they said that they were "close to getting a gravestone for her grave," which they eventually did. Once they completed this part of their grieving process, they were free to go on and confront the other issues in their relationship, which were still there, waiting for them.

To deal with the challenge of the death of a child as Couple, you need to be able to put the past behind you, be grateful for what you have in the present and be flexible enough to create a new future together without that child. As we have seen, that is easier said than done, and as Helene and Josh, another couple grappling with the loss of a child, said, "It is never really done, but you learn to go on and create a life you love together." Helene and Josh, a Dynamic Couple who had been happily married for eight years, had to re-create their life together after a drunk driver hit the car

Helene was driving, killing their only child. While Helene was in the hospital recuperating from her injuries, Josh called upon old friends to come and be with them—friends who had known them before they had a child. They received support from their other friends and family, but they felt that these old friends could help them remember the good times they had had as a couple before they knew themselves as parents. Their old friends came and helped them grieve, and they also helped them remember the joy of their past and create a new future together—one that eventually included four more children.

There is one thing that all the couples described above have in common when confronting the myriad external challenges that life presents: they used the Four C's of Couple Power to invent and implement creative solutions to the outside challenges they faced. That is the secret of lifelong love. The same principles apply to the internal challenges that couples face, as described in the next chapter. First, take some time to assess the external challenges facing your couple.

Exercise: Assessing External Challenges

Spend a half hour or so with your partner reviewing the external challenges you have faced in your relationship.

THINK:	Are there now or have there been external challenges to your relationship? What might they be? Which challenges have you addressed successfully so far using the Four C's of Couple Power? Which ones still need work?
DO:	Make a list of the external challenges in your life. Put a check mark by the ones you have addressed successfully. Place a star by the ones you now want to take on together.

SHARE: Discuss how you will confront the challenges you starred using the Four C's. Look again at the couple vision you created and construct a new couple proclamation, if one is needed.

CHAPTER EIGHT

Applying the Four C's:

Overcoming Internal Challenges to Lifelong Love

*"Real intimacy, in short, brings up our unfinished business—
all the rough spots in ourselves and in our partner that still need
to be polished, refined, and further developed."*

—John Welwood, *Journey of the Heart*

Most of the external challenges we confront—an alcoholic parent or spouse, the death of a parent or child, the illness of a partner or family member—are related to and impact our internal experience, affecting us individually and as a couple. Our internal experience is shaped by the attitudes and beliefs that have been handed down to us from others and by our behaviors and personal histories. Sometimes these attitudes and beliefs are learned very early in life—so early that we may not even be aware that we learned them. Without this awareness, we may not know that we have options and can *unlearn* those attitudes and expectations that do not serve us well, and we can formulate new ones. When we think our attitudes and beliefs are the truth and that our behaviors cannot be changed, that is when our challenges become obstacles, internal challenges, to lifelong love.

In this chapter, we will focus on the internal challenges you may face as a couple, and the strategies that the Four C's of

Couple Power provide for managing them. You may notice an overlap between the internal challenges and some of the external challenges described in Chapter Seven, as they are intricately related. Whether the challenge is external or internal, the most important thing to remember is to work together and employ the Four C's. And don't get pulled into old patterns of blaming each other for your problems. Rather, tackle the challenges as a powerful team facing a "common enemy." No matter what the challenge, you will devise more solutions working as Couple than alone.

Attitudes, Beliefs and Behaviors

Self-centeredness

A behavior or character trait that poses a big challenge for couples is self-centeredness, or narcissism, in one or both partners. When either partner is concerned solely or primarily with his or her own desires, needs or interests, neither partner can be happy for long. The self-centered person usually feels dissatisfied and angry, and his or her partner feels neglected, frustrated and angry as well.

Stan and Sara, the dual-career couple described in Chapter Five and Chapter Seven, had been doing pretty well until Stan lost his job and became extremely agitated and angry. He complained that Sara was too passive and didn't do enough to support him in dealing with his job loss. She told him she felt pressured to fix things for him and felt threatened by his anger. He responded, "I am the one affected here!" In marital therapy they created some strategies for managing Stan's attitude and anger, like exercise, meditation and listening to music. Sara learned to take the initiative more and complete projects she wanted done on her own, like minor home improvements. They committed to several joint projects, including having two date nights a month. The name they gave the job-search project was "Empowered Employment," and they also created a "Beautiful Home" plan. As they began to negotiate and cooperate on these endeavors, Stan became less self-centered and more couple-centered, and the tension that existed between them began to dissipate. The skills they learned in marital therapy carried over into other aspects of their lives, as well, like their sex life. When Stan got a new job, he found he was happier both at home and at work than he'd ever been.

If you are confronted by the challenge of self-centeredness, you may know that it is a deeply engrained behavior and generally takes a strong commitment and considerable time and effort to address. It is often helpful to get some professional help when dealing with self-centeredness, either individually or as a couple, as we discuss at the end of this chapter.

Low self-esteem

While self-centered people are often insecure, they exhibit their insecurity much differently than people with low self-esteem, who tend to be more passive and withdrawn. Those with low self-esteem also do not make many requests or demands, as they may feel they are not worthy enough to ask for something, let alone receive anything of value. Low self-esteem is very damaging not only to the individual but to the couple as well. Implementing the Four C's of Couple Power requires two strong individuals believing in themselves and their relationship. Fortunately, the process of developing a healthy couple generally leads to the development of healthy individuals. That was the case with Helen and Michael, who were discussed in Chapter Five and Chapter Seven.

Helen initially came for therapy because she was depressed about the physical pain she experienced during intercourse and her lack of sexual desire. She thought it was her fault that there were problems with sex in the marriage. Her gynecologist had referred her to Phyllis after finding no physical cause for her pain or her lack of desire. It became clear in the first session of therapy that Helen still had a lot of unresolved anger over the affair Michael had early on in their relationship. In her family and in her culture, women were not supposed to express anger, and she never saw her parents argue, even though they were unhappy; so even acknowledging that she harbored anger was hard for her. It was also difficult for her to ask Michael to come to the therapy sessions with her, as Phyllis suggested, but she did and was able to share some of her feelings with him at the next session.

Michael said that he came to therapy because Helen had asked him to be there. That made her feel more powerful, and she was able to tell him that she felt disconnected from her body and like she was "nothing" sexually because she could not satisfy him. They created the proclamation "We have trust and are closer every day" and started sharing their feelings with each other every day. They continued in couples and sex therapy for the next several months, ultimately creating a mutually satisfying marital and sexual relationship.

Thinking you are not lovable

People with low self-esteem often feel that they are unlovable or unworthy of affection. This belief usually gets instilled very early on in childhood and lasts indefinitely unless it is interrupted in some way. Fortunately, the power of the couple may be instrumental in alleviating this feeling to a great degree. As we said earlier, you don't have to wait until you think you are worthy to be in a relationship. The relationship itself will help you feel lovable. Also, if you feel unlovable even as part of your couple, you don't need to go outside your relationship to try and fill the need to feel loved. However, many people do just that, pursuing sexual affairs. Those affairs are a symptom and a red flag of a more profound problem in the individual and in the couple, not a solution. An affair cannot be justified because a partner feels unlovable. It takes work by the couple, often with outside help, to get to the source of the problem.

Cal and Judy, the Self-Focused Couple described in Chapter Two, became aware of their deeper issues as they dealt with the revelation of Cal's affairs. In therapy, Cal acknowledged his deep longing for acceptance and warmth from his distant parents, who never told him that they loved him. Cal and Judy agreed that this was no excuse for his affairs, but his revelation enabled them both to have more compassion for each other. Judy also saw how she might have contributed to the problem with her frequent sarcastic, cutting remarks to Cal throughout their marriage. They created a new proclamation, "We love each other," and Cal was encouraged to share whenever he felt blamed or cut down by Judy. Soon after that, Judy was able to accept Cal's apology for his affairs and express her forgiveness.

Showing affection

No matter how much you may love your partner, different attitudes about showing affection may create a challenge in your relationship. Some families are very demonstrative in public and in private; some believe that screaming and arguing are ways to show caring. For others, displaying affection is much more private and subtle. These approaches to showing affection are usually internalized early on. If your partner does not express affection in the same way that you do, you may feel rejected, criticized or even under attack. The challenge is to recognize the differences between your styles and communicate them to each other in such a way as to avoid misunderstanding and disconnection.

Uri and Margot, a Romanticized Couple, had been married for one year. They came to therapy after having had a big argument, in which Margot stomped off to their bedroom, crying, and closed the door. Uri, who came from a family where people were private about their feelings, assumed that she wanted to be left alone, so he left the house. When they recounted the incident in a therapy session, Margot said that she felt like he was being cold and callous, that he didn't care about her feelings. Using the "Clearing It Up" exercise, described in Chapter Five, Uri explained what he had really felt. "I didn't want to bother you. I thought you would need time to sort out what you were feeling and that you would ask for my help when you were ready." Margot then revealed, "I did want to pull myself together, but I didn't want you to leave me alone. In times like that, I want your physical support and affection." Uri took her hands in his, and they hugged.

Hugging and kissing may be a common occurrence for you. Many times a hug or a kiss seems almost casual or routine. However, no matter how you show affection to each other in your couple, it is useful and fun to experiment with some new ways of expressing yourselves. For example, try the following exercise.

Exercise: The Seven-Second Kiss

THINK:	How many times do we actually kiss in a given day and in a given week?
DO:	Rather than sharing the usual quick peck on the cheek when you both come home at the end of the day or

when you leave in the morning, try executing a full seven-second kiss on the lips. It's as simple as it sounds, but the intimacy and closeness this kiss creates last much longer than the seven seconds it takes to complete it. Do it once a day for a week.

SHARE: How did the kiss feel? Did seven seconds seem like a long time? A short time? Do you want to keep doing it? Why or why not?

Time management

Another attitude that is often carried over from our families is our attitude about being on time. Some families are scrupulous about being prompt, and others are quite lax about it. Some people follow the time management pattern of their parents, while others, who perhaps found their family's laxity or rigidity frustrating while growing up, may react against it. This may seem like a small issue at first, but attitudes about time management can create a tremendous amount of resentment and anger if not dealt with directly. We had this issue in our own relationship until we worked it out.

We were asked by a friend to participate in a special family celebration. Peter had told Phyllis he wanted to get there early, but Phyllis wasn't ready when he wanted to leave, and we ended up waiting until the last minute to leave the house. When we got to the event, it had already started and we missed the time for our part. Peter was furious, and Phyllis felt very guilty. When we got home, we used this incident as an opportunity to work out our issues about being on time. Phyllis apologized and asked for help in dealing with it, as it had always been a problem with her parents and in her life. Peter agreed to coach her and asked her to keep track of how many times each day she was late or on time. We reviewed the results at the end of each day and discussed how Phyllis could improve her time management. The coaching was very helpful and enabled Phyllis to feel supported in dealing with this challenge. Now she is more generous with Peter when he asks her to be ready to leave early, even if it means getting to the airport two and a half hours before a flight!

If you and your partner have different ideas of what "on time" means, try the following exercise.

Exercise: Making Time Work for You

THINK: What time management issues are you grappling with? What does time mean to each of you? What does being "on time" mean to you: arriving on the dot, less than five minutes late, before an event is over?

DO: Decide what being on time means for each of you. Identify two upcoming events you are going to together where being on time is an issue. Write down in advance when you will leave for the event and when you will arrive at the event. Manage one event according to each person's preferences about time.

SHARE: After the events, discuss what the time schedule was like for each of you. Design a new way to manage time together, try it out and then discuss it.

Fears

At the beginning of the book we discussed the many fears that may keep us from achieving lifelong love. As we've shown, the enemy is not so much the fear itself, but the belief that we cannot overcome it. With the divorce rate in the United States at over 50 percent, it is understandable that many people today fear that a relationship cannot really last or be fulfilling over time. Once you learn and regularly apply the Four C's of Couple Power in your life, however, you will find yourselves becoming more optimistic and confident, especially as you are supported by other couples in similar situations.

The basis of most fears is dealing with change. We get accustomed and attached to things being the way they are, and often resist having them change. But circumstances and people, as we have seen, are not static and will inevitably change over time. While exciting in many ways, change is also challenging, whether it be moving from life as a single person to being part of a couple, or adopting a child or starting a family business. No matter what the situation, these changes bring with them the opportunity for growth. We may not be able to vanquish all our fears about being in a relationship, but we can learn to use them to enhance the intimacy and development of Couple, that entity that is the powerful constant amid all the change. We present here examples of some of these fears and how various couples have overcome them.

Fear of commitment

Much as you may want to be in a relationship, the fear of losing autonomy or independence often conflicts with that desire. You may feel reluctant to take on a long-term commitment as you may believe it could potentially limit your individual choices and interfere with your goals. Thinking about commitment may even bring up associations of being committed or confined to a prison or a mental institution—rather than images of a relationship where both people feel supported in their lives and their work. Coming out of the culture of individualism makes it difficult to shift suddenly to a state of couplism. As one nervous young woman said while shopping for her wedding dress, "This is about more than just a pretty dress and a party. It's a commitment to one person for the rest of my life and everything that comes with that."

That is how it was for us when we first committed to stay together as a couple. Remember that Peter said he was initially very wary of giving up his freedom, but then he finally decided to just "take the plunge." It was similar for Phyllis, who had just gotten her Ph.D. and was finally ready to start her new career. *What if I don't like this job or the city we are moving to?* she thought. Plus, she was just getting over a failed marriage and was afraid of making a "mistake" and failing at another marriage. Then she imagined a future of having children with Peter and felt inspired and excited. "It was a decision of the heart," she said. We could look at the pros and cons forever, but it wasn't about that. We came to see that it was about the future that we wanted to create together. Or, as a friend of ours described her decision to marry the man who is now her husband of over thirty years, "It was more important to see what would happen on that journey together than not to take the risk."

Those who have been divorced tend to have more intense fears of committing to a marriage than those who have not. The fears may be well-founded, because, in fact, statistics show that if you have been divorced, you are more likely to get divorced again. This may be because you are expecting it or find it easier to get divorced the next time, or you haven't learned from your mistakes. Have no fear, however, for acknowledging the fears and working on them is likely to increase your chances of achieving success and lifelong love the second (or third or however many) time around.

Ben and Belinda, a Traditional Couple in their fifties, had both recently divorced after long marriages. They fell in love and began Couples Coaching Couples, with Robert and Laura as their first coaches. When they were asked about their plans for marriage, Belinda said she was looking for her "soul mate"—and Ben didn't seem to fit the bill. When she was coached to look deeper, she saw that she was actually stuck in her fear of getting into another bad relationship that would be hard to leave. Ben said that he thought he was ready to make a commitment, but like Belinda, he felt like he had been "burned" before. Ben was afraid of being hurt and "losing my money again." Robert and Laura pointed out to them that their agonizing over the decision to commit could go on forever.

The homework assigned to Ben and Belinda was to discover what they truly wanted for their couple. They asked some other couples they knew how they had decided to get married. They spent some time discussing what they heard and got inspired to consider what they truly wanted for their own relationship. In doing this, they got in touch with their vision of forming a loving friendship and partnership with each other for life. They created the proclamation "We are fearlessly and joyfully discovering new horizons as Couple." After fourteen years of marriage, they are still in CCC and tell everyone that "Couple is our strength."

It is always a risk to make the change from being alone to committing to be part of a couple. You may lose some freedom, but the sacrifice is probably worth it, as many studies have shown that married people are generally happier than unmarried people. Being aware of your fears and feelings about giving up your life alone, however, is the first step in helping you deal with them. In this regard, you may want to think about what you would be doing and thinking now if you were not in a committed relationship. The exercise below, "If I Were Alone," may help you recognize your own fears and identify some of the personal barriers that are preventing you from making a full commitment to your relationship. As you discuss the exercise together with your partner, you might be surprised to see that you face fewer barriers to lifelong love than you thought.

Exercise: If I Were Alone

THINK:	If you weren't in a couple right now—and you had no shared responsibilities or child-care duties—how would you like to spend your time?
DO:	On a blank sheet of paper, list ten things you would do this week if you were not in a relationship. Have your partner make a separate list of ten things s/he would do.
SHARE:	Compare your lists. Do they have anything in common? What things are different? Talk about the differences between your lists. Are there things that you thought of that you would do alone that you might do with your partner? Why or why not? Do you see things on your partner's list that you would be willing to participate in with him or her?

Fear of intimacy

Once a commitment has been made, the fear that next comes up for many people is a fear of closeness or intimacy. Fear of intimacy, both physical and emotional, is inherent in all relationships, and it is often especially powerful in a couple relationship with its close physical and emotional connections. Psychotherapist John

Welwood, author of *Journey of the Heart,* says that "the deeper a soul connection is, the more it brings out the best and the worst in us.... We begin to experience our deepest fears, insecurities, and resistance to intimacy." There is no optimal degree of intimacy for all couples, as each relationship and each individual is emotionally and physiologically unique. Each of us has our distinct preferences for closeness, affection and touch. We all need a sense that our own personal space and our inner core are safe and secure. What is required is for us to strike a balance between autonomy and intimacy. How this is done varies from couple to couple.

Belinda and Tony were recently married. Both were in their early sixties. Tony's first marriage, which lasted twenty-five years, had ended in divorce. Belinda, a former nun, had never been married. They said they were drawn to each other in a very powerful way but weren't sure how to express their intimacy. Belinda had been celibate for nearly twenty-five years but was now interested in resuming the sex life she had known as a teenager. Tony was not sure how to respond. He was actually less interested in sex per se and more interested in the emotional connection he felt with her. He was happy to spend time with her just talking, walking and traveling. She was disappointed and felt she was not attractive enough to spark his sexual interest. He felt pressured, and she felt unloved. Each thought the other had a superficial notion of what intimacy was.

Peter worked with them in couples therapy on sharing what intimacy felt like for them. He asked them to make a list of all the ways they could achieve these feelings. He suggested that they invent some new "experiments" in intimacy. They alternated between each other's experiments (showering together, going to a racy nightclub, staying up all night watching romantic movies on television) and then discussed how they felt about them. They did these experiments monthly and especially enjoyed the time they spent together discussing their experiences. Over time, they learned that there were many more ways to experience intimacy with each other than they had first thought.

Fear of being vulnerable or being rejected

Once in an intimate relationship, you may fear being vulnerable to your partner. *If I really open myself up to this person I love, what will I do if they hurt or reject me?* you might think. If your partner gets angry or critical, you may feel rejected. You may be afraid that your partner does not like what s/he sees. The challenge is not to let these fears inhibit your honest self-expression and authentic communication. It is often difficult to bring up such feelings, and often they operate in the background, subconsciously. If not recognized and dealt with, however, they might diminish the strength of your commitment to your relationship.

The first step in dealing with your fear of being vulnerable or rejected, then, is to be aware of the fear and acknowledge it to yourself. If you notice you are holding back on sharing your innermost feelings with your partner, stop and ask yourself what is hindering you. Are you afraid of being ignored or criticized or even attacked or abandoned? Do these feelings occur in your fantasies or your dreams? You may have been preventing yourself from recognizing that these fears were there so as not to have to deal with them. We call this denial. It doesn't work well. Awareness is the key to open the door to change.

Certainly, if there is a risk of physical or emotional abuse, you need to acknowledge that and take action to protect yourself. Otherwise, you need to take the next step, which is working on building up courage to face your fears and acknowledge them to your partner. This step is essential to lifelong love. Remember the commitment you have to your relationship. That is the cornerstone of facing your fear together. Ask your partner to agree to listen to you without interrupting or criticizing you. Then make some agreements to share your feelings with each other in a way that you both feel safe.

Caren and Phil, a Dynamic Couple who had each been married before, set out to create a marriage that would be deeply satisfying and would give both of them the support and the space they needed for the rest of their lives. A cornerstone of their marriage was an agreement not to suppress their feelings when there was something important that they were afraid to say to the other. When they stepped beyond their fear of saying something that might hurt the other person, they didn't experience the upset or retaliation they feared, but rather deeper intimacy. Their approach was to listen to such statements as acts of vulnerability, as gifts of intimacy, and rather than defending themselves, to ask, "Is there more?"

Exercise: Is There More?

THINK:	What are some feelings or areas of your life that you have not shared with your partner? Think about what is stopping you from sharing them.
DO:	Make a list of those feelings or areas of your life that you have not shared with your partner. Choose one feeling or area to share with your partner. Find an appropriate place and time to do that.
SHARE:	Say your couple proclamation together first to honor your commitment and to create a safe space. Then

share with your partner the feeling or area you chose from your list. Allow your partner to respond and then discuss your reactions. Invite your partner to share something that went unsaid with you then or now.

Assessing Your Challenges

You may have noticed when reading about the external and internal challenges that couples face that in overcoming them, all the couples had one thing in common: they all were committed to something beyond their own feelings. The first step in getting beyond your feelings is recognizing them. Then you may use the tools of the Four C's of Couple Power to meet these challenges together. Start by doing the following exercise if you are confronting an internal challenge.

Exercise: Assessing Internal Challenges

Spend a half hour or so with your partner reviewing the internal challenges and how they apply to your relationship.

THINK:	Which challenges have you addressed successfully so far using the Four C's of Couple Power? Which ones still need work?
DO:	Make a list of the internal challenges in your life. Put a check mark by the ones you have addressed successfully. Place a star by the ones you now want to take on together.

> **SHARE:** Look again at the vision you have created for your relationship and create a new couple proclamation, if one is needed.

When to Get Professional Help

In assessing the internal and external challenges in your couple's life, you may feel that you are not able or ready yet to manage them using the tools of the Four C's of Couple Power. It could be that you don't have enough practice or that you are too distracted by other stresses. It might be that your life has been so busy that you have not taken your relationship seriously. Many of us just assume that if there is true love, we will know what to do all the time. Loving and feeling loved by your partner definitely help, but love is not enough. As with many areas of life, we acquire more information as we go along, and what we assumed in the beginning sometimes turns out to need modification.

You may have a sense that things could be better in your relationship and that professional help is necessary to get there. But when is the right time to seek it out? You probably don't want to broach the topic too soon if you think that the problems might clear up on their own or that the stressors creating your problems might go away over time—things like financial pressure, grief and loss, and work transitions. If you wait too long to seek professional help, however, it may be too late to recuperate or reclaim your couple.

So when is the right time? Like your decision to go to the doctor or not when you are sick, your decision to find a therapist or counselor should hinge on the degree of pain and suffering you are enduring. When the pain is so great that you have trouble functioning, that is, doing your daily tasks, sleeping and eating, it is time to seek help. The right time might also be when you and your partner notice a significant increase in arguing, drinking, violence, isolation or sadness in your relationship. There may be a particular incident or moment that tells you it is time to act—a "red flag," such as discovering an affair or hearing a negative comment about your relationship from another person. As with medical conditions, the decision to seek help often occurs much later than is advisable. In a couple, there is sometimes a hesitation that comes from neither of you wanting to take full responsibility for taking action. You may wait for your partner to act first and wind up putting off a decision longer and longer. Based on our more than thirty years of experience as therapists and having treated thousands of couples, we believe that the best time to get outside help is when you *first* notice the problem, not when it's gotten so bad that you think the damage to the relationship is irreparable. At the same time, it's *never* too late to get help.

It is not unreasonable to consider having a "couple checkup," similar to an annual physical. Speak with friends or clergy about your couple, or sign up for a marriage enrichment program that includes assessing the current status of your relationship. The results of your "couple checkup" may indicate that some help is needed. Don't feel that dramatic intervention is always necessary. You may want to participate in couples counseling or therapy a little at a time for extra help or just for enrichment.

Listed below are some of the most common reasons that couples seek counseling.

Blended families and remarriage

Whenever there is a change in the structure of the family or the couple, stress is placed on the entire family system. Losing a partner, getting divorced and remarried, bringing together children from two relationships and sharing custody of children with other people are all significant stressors, and the impact they have on a relationship may motivate a couple to consider evaluation or treatment.

Blended families have unique issues related to communication and couple functioning: stepchildren who don't like their new stepparent, stepkids who don't like each other, exes who interfere, exes who don't pull their weight with child care or finances. In addition to the challenges of financial planning, legal matters, child rearing, holidays and visitation rights, the couple has to deal with the children's adjustment to the absence of one parent and the integration of a stepparent into the family. The impact on the couple may be intense, and problems may arise that are difficult to resolve. Involving a professional often helps to provide a base of support for the new couple to work together on the issues as a team. They can take a "time-out" and go to their "coach" for help in developing a new game plan. Without that outside support, it is often too hard to see the forest for the trees. You are too involved in the problem to see new possibilities. That is what a professional can help your couple do.

Sexual issues and dysfunction

Sex and sexual functioning are viewed by most of us as the cornerstone of a good relationship. In fact, our expectations about this facet of our relationship are so incredibly high that we will almost certainly fall short or fail. Learning to understand what is "normal" is very difficult. What is normal varies a great deal from person to person and couple to couple. Managing expectations is very important when it comes to many things, but especially sexual functioning. Most people believe that if they are in love and in a solid relationship, sex should automatically be enjoyable and frequent. That is not always the case, however. Positive sexual functioning and performance are, like many behaviors, learned.

For most people, what is essential is not the particular erotic behaviors, but whether or not they are gratifying. In order to know what is satisfying for each partner, a certain amount of communication is necessary. However, communication about sexual satisfaction is often difficult. As we said earlier, we barely even have a language to speak about it that is not medical, euphemistic or crude. Therapy may enable a couple to develop good communication about sex—even during sex—especially when commitment exists. Figuring out that there is a real problem in need of medical or psychological intervention requires that those involved share information about their experience with each other and with professionals. A brief program of sex therapy with a therapist specifically trained in this area may prove very helpful in this regard, especially in cases that involve such issues as erectile dysfunction, premature ejaculation, painful sex and inhibited sexual desire.

Several specific sex therapy programs based on the behavioral principles and studies of Masters and Johnson exist, and homework exercises are an integral part of them. Exercises, such as massage and sensate focus, are quite helpful in desensitizing uncomfortable physical areas and can teach you more about your own and your partner's body. While doing these exercises, you learn to experience and appreciate each other's bodies and share your sensual reactions more openly. Even physiological sexual problems are able to be treated and, if not completely cured, may be minimized to such a degree that a wonderful, lasting relationship is possible. The experience of Helen and Michael, discussed in Chapter Five, Chapter Seven and earlier in this chapter, is a case in point. By the end of their experience with couples and sex therapy, they were living their proclamation of being "joyfully blissed out."

Affairs

Sometimes affairs are the offshoot of something that has been going wrong for the couple: one partner seeks to remedy the perceived deficit they see in their current partner by getting involved with someone else. It may also be, however, that the affair has less to do with finding a better person than experiencing the freedom of being with someone intimately when not under the pressure of home life, family or finances. The affairs may now be virtual, conducted entirely in cyberspace. When an affair has happened, couples often seek treatment to figure out whether or not there is enough commitment and love left to stay in the relationship. Commitment to the relationship, of course, requires the partner who strayed to give up the affair. Professional counseling can help couples learn how to take on the problem of the affair together. The example of Cal and Judy in Chapter Two is a good example of getting past the trauma of an affair and creating a fulfilling relationship.

Violence and fear of violence

Violence and threats of violence are a sure sign of the need for outside help. No amount of work on the relationship will be effective or lasting until this issue is handled. There must be a safe environment in order to create and maintain a fulfilling relationship. The environment is not safe if any type of violence or threat of violence occurs, whether it be physical (hitting, shoving, restraining, throwing objects), sexual or emotional (intimidation, controlling or domineering behavior). These kinds of behaviors affect couples across society, regardless of gender or economic status, and involve over 10 percent of the U.S. population. If violence or the threat of violence occurs in your relationship, it is important to get help and tell your therapist about all the circumstances involved, no matter how difficult it is to talk about. That is what Stan and Sara, the dual-career couple mentioned in Chapter Five and Chapter Seven, did. Sara was frightened by Stan's angry outbursts. When she brought it up in therapy, they were able to address the issue directly and work out ways to control the situation and allow her to feel safe.

Substance abuse

Alcohol and drug use are difficult issues in relationships for a number of reasons. One is the impact of these substances on people's health in general, and another is that intoxication may cause people to distort or ignore reality in a dangerous way. Sometimes one partner is a user or abuser and the other is not, but in other cases both partners are users, and it keeps them from being honest or forthright with each other. They use drugs or alcohol to escape from conflict or disagreements, and the substance abuse may disinhibit them, creating more conflict or dangerous behaviors.

Substance abuse makes couple treatment difficult. Until the abuse is halted, a true commitment to Couple cannot be made, and any progress may be sabotaged. If addiction is currently a factor for either of you, Alcoholics Anonymous or Narcotics Anonymous or other twelve step programs are a good alternative or adjunct to treatment. Whether one or both of you gets treatment for addiction, you both operate with Couple supporting the treatment.

Doubt about commitment

For some couples, therapy is a way to explore whether to stay together or to separate. In our practice, we have found that in a certain number of couples, one of the partners has already decided to leave but seeks justification or agreement from the therapist that they are doing the correct thing. These partners often have not been honest with their spouse, withholding the fact that they have already decided to leave the relationship. They might be concerned about hurting the other person, or they might be fearful of their partner's response. A third party in these instances is very helpful. In these cases, it may be possible to explore what is needed for the partners to stay together, but most often therapy is an opportunity to get help with how to separate in a way that is least painful for all parties. This often includes how to support and deal with children and other family members. Mediation may be helpful in addressing some of the legal and financial issues related to divorce and the custody of children.

What Kind of Help to Get

Treatment may take many forms, and there are many different kinds of professionals who provide it. You may want to begin by asking trusted friends if they have a recommendation of where to get professional help. There are also professional referral services and professional associations (of psychologists, social workers, counselors, physicians and even collaborative attorneys) that provide information about treatment options. Churches, synagogues and mosques often have resources or pastoral counselors who can assess, treat and refer couples. Health professionals and your health insurance company can provide assistance in locating resources and venues for professional help.

When choosing treatment, don't be afraid to shop around. Finding the right person, program or treatment approach is very important. There is no one-size-fits-all treatment. If you don't find what you want right away, keep looking. Be sure, however, that you are willing to commit to doing some work. And don't use shopping around as an excuse to avoid choosing anything. Remember that a good relationship is like gold. Even a little of it is worth hanging on to. A good relationship can be the foundation of energy, power, contentment and lifelong love. So seek help when necessary to nurture your relationship.

CHAPTER NINE

Beyond the Four C's

"We shall not cease from exploration
And the end of all our exploring
Will be to arrive where we started
And know the place for the first time."

—T. S. Eliot, "Little Gidding"

In many ways, this is a remarkable era in the history of marriage and couple relationships. The profound cultural drift away from a commitment to relationships toward individualistic concerns, described in Chapter Seven, seems to be leading us to the brink of chronic emotional isolation. While the idea of being in a relationship continues to be attractive to almost everyone, the prospect of actually living this way on a daily basis often seems frightening, difficult and risky. As we have seen, relationships are fraught with legal, emotional and cultural hazards. Many people today begin relationships by making sure there is a way out. It may seem like being in a committed couple is all work and no play, and that we have to spend all our time just trying to make things work out and get along.

What we may not realize is that living beyond the basics of just getting along requires not so much effort as *awareness*—an awareness of what's currently there and then envisioning what's *possible*. It is possible to look ahead, to have a positive vision of a future together, a future in which the feelings we felt when we were most in love are present. We might require some outside help to produce that vision, as discussed in Chapter Eight, or some additional education or some new experiences. At first, we tend to look "inside the box" we are in to try to make things different or better. That is hard work and usually doesn't lead to lasting change. There is, however another way: simply step "outside of the box" you are accustomed to and create something brand-new, something even beyond the Four C's. But why would we want to do this? Because commitment, cooperation, communication and community provide the *foundation* for exceptional relationships and lifelong love. Just look at the stories of many of the couples in this book. What becomes clear is that more may be possible for you and your relationship than you have ever imagined.

Usually we are focused on making our own relationship work and avoiding problems. However, there is something to be learned by being concerned not only with ourselves but with other couples as well. We have examined the power of community in supporting our relationships. When we operate as a healthy and happy couple, it is not just for ourselves, but for our children, and we are also an example, a beacon for others to follow, a declaration that such relationships can, in fact, exist. Though we may not be aware of it, other people, our friends or acquaintances, may see this more clearly and even be inspired by it.

Sometimes a couple starts acting like an "individual" in relation to others and becomes closed, rigid or self-serving. "We can handle our problems by ourselves," some couples say. We described earlier the potential destructive effects of individualism on a couple. The same thing can happen over time when a couple itself becomes more like "an individual." If we get too absorbed in our own relationship, we risk having it become stagnant. It is unable to grow, expand or flourish. When that happens, a sense of community and connectedness to others is lost. We saw in Chapter Six how crucial the connection to community is to maintaining lifelong love. This connectedness requires going beyond our own couple. It requires a change in our perspective—and a vision of what the world would look like if we began to believe that relationships can succeed most of the time, rather than fail.

We will examine expanding our awareness of the power of Couple itself. Shifting the focus of a relationship from the individual to the entity Couple will truly change your view of the world and the daily experience of being in your couple. It is not that the world will change; it is that *you* will change. It is not how the world is, but how you choose to see it. "We shall not cease from exploration," as T. S. Eliot says. The journey is not about finding a new place, however, but understanding that we have a choice about the place we're in and exercising that choice powerfully. That place is the space of relationships, the experience of couple. The choice is lifelong love.

Couple Consciousness—The Fifth C

Once you have learned and mastered the principles of the Four C's of Couple Power, with or without outside help, as discussed in Chapter Eight, you can turn your attention to a final concept, one built upon the foundation of the Four C's. Its mastery will enable lifelong love to remain alive in your relationship and will open up a new world for your couple. This concept, this Fifth C, is what we call "couple consciousness," a way of looking at yourself, your partner and the world through the eyes of Couple. It is the foundation of partnership deep within Couple; it is the paradigm shift from individualism to "couplism," from "me-ness" to "we-ness." After a while, couple consciousness becomes a routine way of thinking and being in everything you do. It is like a lens or filter through which you see the world. Instead of having to agonize over every decision, you will think, *How does this serve* us, *not just me?* Life becomes easier and more joyful with the worldview of Couple. It is a place to come from in whatever you do. Possibilities, options and visions may be created for anything you encounter in your life, from small events to big problems. It starts with looking at your own relationship and then creating possibilities together that can make a difference for others. There are many examples of couples doing this—and making a significant impact on both their personal and professional lives. Here are two of our favorites.

Ed and Angela had been married for twenty-seven years. They had two sons, ages twenty-two and twenty. When Ed retired from the military, he became a youth minister for a large local church. At the time Ed and Angela met, they had the vision of doing things together as much as possible. It was "natural," Angela reported, to give up her career as a journalist and begin working as an administrator in the church where Ed was a youth minister. Soon, however, they both began feeling stressed by their heavy workloads and difficulties that developed with Angela's health. Shortly thereafter, Angela was diagnosed with MS. She felt little community support then from the people "who only knew me as healthy," she said. She wanted to move to a smaller town; Ed wanted to work on adjusting to where they were. However, he soon saw, as he later reported, that they were "a better couple" when Angela was doing well. At that point, they decided to trust in their couple. Ed quit his job, and they moved to a smaller town with an active MS chapter and a good hospital. After the move, Angela quickly began to regain her confidence, and "We could hear each other again," they said.

Angela and Ed then took on dealing with her MS as a team, asking for help from colleagues and friends who had noticed their close interaction and were inspired by their example. "Knowing that people are affected by who we are," they reported, "makes us want to be even better. We value being part of a community organized around a task and a mission based on acceptance and caring. We see that taking on something bigger than yourself strengthens your couple and that the community can also give back to you." Angela and Ed are truly an inspiration, despite their adversities. They represent what they saw in each other when they first got together. Angela said, "I always told him 'You're my hero,' and he always said, 'You're my inspiration.'" Being that for each other allowed them to think outside the box, create a powerful couple vision and make a profound difference in the lives of nearly everyone around them.

Issac, a physician, and Suja, an educator and nutritionist, got married three months after their parents introduced them to each other. Their relationship was arranged. When Issac asked Suja to marry him, he told her he wanted her support in developing his dream of having a health center in India. "I chose to join his dream," Suja said, "our couple dream." In the beginning, they were both involved in all aspects of the health center, including its design, name, logo, finances and the hiring of staff. Later on, they divided the tasks, with Suja being in charge of the administration and nutrition, and Issac taking on the medical and financial responsibilities. Though they did not have fixed meetings, they discussed everything about the operation of the center informally. While they were planning the center, which was a long process, they had three children and opened two charity clinics.

After thirteen years of marriage and planning, they opened their health center, Soukya, which means "well-being" and "a harmonious state of mind, body and spirit." They have a large staff of people, who are "like part of our family," they reported. The entire operation is an example of the Four C's in action: it is based on a commitment to their vision of healing for all, guests and staff alike; everyone cooperates, starting with a daily morning meeting of all staff. Open communication at all levels is encouraged, with positive criticism and appreciation being the standard for both their couple and the center. Community is present and encouraged among the staff and with the guests through ongoing educational, recreational and cultural activities at the center. The success of Isaac and Suja's relationship is based, they say, on "not expecting the other person to fit into your mold and not taking each other for granted." To themselves and to those who interact with them, they are clearly and deeply in love.

Issac and Suja, as well as Angela and Ed, demonstrate the Four C's and couple consciousness in everything they do—in their work, in their family and with their friends. They provide support to others and each other through who they are as Couple, and their community provides support to them, which continually empowers their family and benefits their work. The application of this kind of couple consciousness to the world we live in, as we can see from these examples, has huge implications for our future and that of our children and grandchildren. Imagine the legacy of this kind of love and connection six or seven generations from now. Lifelong love is the possibility of many different forms of relationship being successful. The standard of measurement does not have to be other relationships or the norms of society, but whether you are acting in accordance with your own vision. This is the key to successful couples and successful societies—that people are willing to stand up for preserving what they created.

This way of relating requires proclaiming what you are committed to, which is different from just talking about it. "Talking about" something is just describing it. Like the Declaration of Independence and the Emancipation Proclamation demonstrate, proclaiming is the act of committing to something as a possibility or a vision and working to make it a reality. It is this kind of speaking that we engaged in when we had a conversation with a friend of ours who was then a member of the U.S. Congress. We speculated with him about what it might be like for us to hold political office as Couple. He said, "Oh, you mean that you would divide up the work and responsibilities?" We said, "No, we would actually hold the seat as Couple, working together on issues and seeing them through a couple view of the world. We would look at how legislation or government actions might support couples and families, not just individuals. We would look at issues of war, peace, economic development and world harmony through the eyes of a couple in a healthy relationship, not just those of an individual."

The Four C's of Couple Power—and the Fifth C, couple consciousness—are applicable to any kind of relationship or organization. Putting those tools to work might lead to a whole new kind of world, one that operates with commitment and caring, rather than suspicion and fear, as the basis for human interaction. We cannot have peace and freedom without responsible action to maintain it. Couple Power is something you create; it doesn't just happen to you. As Erich Fromm states in *The Art of Loving*, "Important and radical changes in our social structure are necessary, if love is to become a social and not a highly individualistic, marginal phenomenon."

Couple as an Oasis

Couple consciousness makes a difference both inwardly for each partner and outwardly into the world, empowering individuals, families and communities to achieve lifelong love and their visions for themselves and others. Like an oasis, this way of being can provide refuge, relief and creativity.

Couple consciousness inward

Rather than being limited or constrained by Couple, as many people are afraid will happen, it is possible to profit and grow through the power of our relationships. Although some of us may initially be afraid of losing our identity or freedom in a committed relationship, we find that this is not the case when Couple is seen as the source of power for each partner, not a limitation or a compromise. You may think that to be part of a couple, you have to give up who you are as an individual. In fact, we have found that individual identity and individuation are actually strengthened when Couple is present. As theologian Thomas Merton once said, "We discover our true selves in love." This is how it was for Angela, mentioned above, as she quickly regained her self-confidence once she and Ed started trusting their couple again. In addition, Ed reported that he "had to grow as he learned to appreciate her more." This kind of individual growth was also true for Helen and Michael, the couple in marital and sex therapy mentioned in previous chapters.

In the beginning of therapy, Helen was depressed and withdrawn, unwilling to share her true feelings or assert herself. She even said one day that she felt like she was "nothing." Helen and Michael agreed to work together on the issues she was facing in their relationship and created the proclamation "We talk and listen with all our hearts and all our might." Michael started listening to Helen more and became more empathetic and patient with her, and Helen began trusting that she could be herself with him. She started speaking up and giving her opinions to Michael and to others. Gradually, Helen noticed that as Michael showed more respect for her opinions, she was able to trust him more and respect herself as well. She even started telling Michael what she liked sexually, increasing the joy and satisfaction available to both of them.

Couple consciousness outward

Couple consciousness, once a part of us, will extend naturally into our surrounding environment. The Couples Coaching Couples community is keenly aware of this. According to the CCC Manual, "As a great river may begin from a small trickle of melting ice or group of streams, so, too, the source of all relationships is Couple." Two final examples serve to illustrate this principle.

Laura and Robert, whose experiences are described in Chapter Two and Chapter Three, demonstrated the expansive power of Couple, even at the end of Robert's life. Robert was diagnosed with a terminal illness, and when he was in the final stages, they invited all three of Robert's children from a past marriage for a weekend family reunion of sorts. They spoke as Couple about their intention to provide the opportunity for everyone to communicate whatever they needed to say and to be complete with their father while he was still alive. All of them agreed at the outset that each person would have as much time as s/he needed to speak, while the others simply listened with an open heart and mind.

Many tears were shed as the emotional undercurrents began to shift from hurt and blame to compassion and caring. When everyone felt fully heard, it became clear that all the negative energy was gone, and the space was cleared and open to love. It was the strength of the example of Robert and Laura's love that was a catalyst for his children to forgive him for everything in the past—his drinking, his leaving them when he divorced their mother and not being the perfect father. Two years later, at the end of Robert's life, it was the collective strength of the family, created that weekend by Robert and Laura, that supported Laura through her grief. Soon she was able to move on with her life, developing other relationships and carrying the pleasant memory of that support with her. It is clear from Robert and Laura's experience that couple consciousness can alter how we approach some very difficult situations in life. In their case, as their couple was empowered to deal with their own issues, they were able to give the gift of responsible listening to their children as well.

Being a model of couple consciousness that inspires others is one way for Couple to be a source of strength to our families and communities. We frequently recall a difficult situation in our own life when this way of thinking made a meaningful difference to us and our young children. Peter's dad was diagnosed with terminal cancer, and we both knew it was just a matter of time before we would have to face his death. To a great extent, we dreaded making what we knew would be the final trip to visit him. It seemed as though we were spending most of our energy just supporting each other and the children to "get through" what we expected would be a stressful journey. We realized we needed a new way to think about it all. We thought about who we wanted to be as Couple and as a family, and we began to see another way of looking at the trip: instead of having a stressful, depressing and sad visit, what if we made it into something enjoyable for all of us? The reason for making the visit was sad, but the actual visit didn't have to be. We realized that Grandpa would much rather have a happy family visiting him than one that looked stricken, stressed out and morose. Rather than anticipating our loss, we could choose to be happy together in the moment.

We flew to the city closest to the hospital and rented a luxury car to make the two-hour drive. We stopped on the way to shop for toys at the outlet mall and play miniature golf. We had a wonderful time getting to the hospital. When we arrived for visiting hours, we were all in a great mood. Just being around all of us, Grandpa perked up. Within a day, he started eating, talking and feeling well enough to go back home. During the visits that followed over the next few days, we sat and ate together, told family stories and played cards. We all just had fun together. Just before we left, Grandpa took a Polaroid picture of us standing at the foot of his bed, laughing and smiling. We taped the picture there at the foot of the bed. He later told Grandma that looking at that picture made him feel like we had never left.

Grandpa died around Halloween that year, but we all felt we had seen him at his best. His doctor and Grandma both said that he probably lived longer because we were there, and that he was content until the end. At the funeral the whole family remembered our trip a few months before, and we laughed as we looked at the picture we had left behind. We were able to have an exceptional experience with him. Because our couple was present to love, we had designed a journey together of joy and laughter, a memory we will always cherish.

And so, once you have learned the Four C's of Couple Power, you may master the Fifth C, expanding your own couple's consciousness by sharing your visions and victories with others in your family and community. The power of being a model for those around you cannot be overestimated. Sharing these things makes maintaining lifelong love more probable. For example, consider participating in your church, your neighborhood or a service organization as a model of a couple who is working effectively together and having fun in the process. One couple we know went out and worked with a local community organization to create educational programs in relationship building and responsible parenting for young adults. Simply organizing gatherings for your extended family or for other couples, such as the Thanksgiving dinner that Kali and Dudley arranged for both their families, described in Chapter Six, helps spread the joy of Couple.

As with a fallow garden, fixed in place for a long time, we break up the soil to promote growth. The soil is then fertilized by the residue from our previous couple patterns and behaviors. We may use what we learned from the old patterns and behaviors to create new ones for the future, to nurture Couple and help it grow. If the fertilizer is merely spread on top of the ground and left there, like unresolved issues in a couple, it may stifle growth. If tilled into the soil, however, on a continuing basis, like daily recitation of the couple proclamation, it will foster the creation of new growth that may feed many people. Maybe relationships don't need "fixing"; they merely need fertilizing.

Exercise: Fertilizing Your Couple Garden

THINK: Think about how to fertilize your own couple "garden." Look at how the lives of those around you would be different if you were functioning consistently as a Dynamic Couple. Imagine what the world would look like if your couple proclamations were true for all couples. What actions would be necessary in your community to make that happen? Look for examples in your couple of couple consciousness, both inward and outward.

DO:	Come up with one action you could take to express couple consciousness inwardly for your partner, and then do that. Next, devise an action to take as Couple that would express couple consciousness outwardly in your family or community, and do that.
SHARE:	Talk together about how those actions turned out, that is, how they impacted your partner and your family and community, and how it felt to be the source of that.

Conclusion: Looking into the Future

Now we are here, at "the end of all our exploring," as T. S. Eliot said. We have arrived "where we started," with being related and we "know the place for the first time." With a thorough knowledge of and the regular practice of the Four C's of Couple Power, we are able to create Couple, the place of basic connection. Since there is no right or wrong way to be, the important thing is finding what is most satisfying for your couple at any particular moment in your life. "We shall not cease from exploration," since the creation and maintenance of lifelong love is an ongoing process. The process of creating and maintaining lifelong love also involves, as we have seen, clearing out the obstacles that may be blocking the way of Couple—our attitudes, fears, attachments, expectations, cultural standards and so on. What it takes is being willing to face these obstacles and commit yourselves to something bigger and more valuable, that is, your couple vision and what it makes possible for you—and others.

Like anything important that we are committed to maintaining in our life, Couple takes constant attention and practice. If we ignore it for too long, the "weeds" will take over, and the "plants" will go to seed. Lifelong love is something we continuously create; it doesn't just happen to us. So just *knowing* the Four C's is not enough. We must experience them in our life on a daily basis, by performing personal rituals, holding celebrations and revitalizing couple visions and proclamations. Once we let go of the obstacles to the basic reality of connection, we are free to experience the power of that connection in our couple forever. The key is to keep practicing and sharing. Others will benefit along the way, as will we. Lifelong love is a journey, not just a destination. Enjoy the trip!

Bibliography

Beck, Aaron T. *Love Is Never Enough*. New York: Harper & Row, 1988.

Berne, Eric. *Transactional Analysis in Psychotherapy*. New York: Ballantine, 1961.

Cohen, Leonard. "Dance Me to the End of Love." *Various Positions*. Rounder Records, 1995.

de La Rochefoucauld, François. *Collected Maxims and Other Reflections*. New York: Oxford University Press, 2008.

Doss, B., J. Jones, and A. Christensen. "Integrative Behavioral Couples Therapy." *Comprehensive Handbook of Psychotherapy*, vol. 4, ed. J. Lebow. New York: Wiley, 2002.

Eliot, T. S. "Little Gidding." *Four Quartets*. New York: Harcourt, Brace and World, Inc., 1943.

Fowers, Blaine J. *Beyond the Myth of Marital Happiness*. San Francisco: Jossey-Bass, 2000.

Frankl, Viktor E. *Man's Search for Meaning*. Boston: Beacon Press, 1992.

Jung, Carl G. *The Red Book*, ed. Sonu Shamdasni. W.W. Norton & Co., 2009.

Miriam-Webster's Collegiate Dictionary—11th Edition. Springfield, MA: Miriam-Webster, Inc., 2004.

The National Marriage Project. "The State of Our Unions—Marriage in America: Money and Marriage." Broadway Publications, 2009.

Peck, M. Scott. *The Different Drum: Community Making and Peace.* New York: Simon & Schuster, 1987.

Rodriguez, Gregory. "Prepare Ourselves for a Boom of an Entirely Different Sort." *Los Angeles Times.* July 13, 2009.

Sheras, Peter L., and Phyllis R. Koch-Sheras. *Couple Power Therapy: Building Commitment, Cooperation, Communication, and Community in Relationships.* Washington, DC: American Psychological Association, 2006.

Stanley, Scott M. *The Power of Commitment: A Guide to Active, Lifelong Love.* San Francisco: Jossey-Bass, 2005.

Welwood, John. *Journey of the Heart.* New York: HarperCollins, 1990.

Index